Dr Emma-Louise Emerson

Falls Prevention and Recovery

The Ultimate Guide for Equestrians

First published in Great Britain in 2024

Copyright © Dr Emma-Louise Emerson
The moral right of the author has been asserted.
All rights reserved.

No part of this publication may be reproduced, stored in a retrieval system, or transmitted, in any form or by any means, without the prior permission in writing of the publisher, nor be otherwise circulated in any form of binding or cover other than that in which it is published and without a similar condition including this condition being imposed on the subsequent purchaser.

Editing, typesetting and publishing by UK Book Publishing

www.ukbookpublishing.com

ISBN: 978-1-917329-12-5

Table of Contents

Chapter 1: Introbuction	1
Chapter 2: Horse Riding Safety	7
Chapter 3: Fall Recovery (It Takes A Village)	12
Chapter 4: The Truth About Concussion	18
Chapter 5: Understanding And Recovering From Whiplash For Horse Riders	22
Chapter 6: Children And Falls – Risks And Rewards	27
Chapter 7: Safety Standards: Best Practice And The Law	35
Chapter 8: How To Prepare For Falls	40
Chapter 9: The Physics Behind Falling	51
Chapter 10: The Neuroscience Of Healing	59
Chapter 11: The Natural Inflammatory Cascade - Should We Really Be Trying To Avoid Inflammation?	70
Chapter 12: Rebuilding Confidence After A Fall	79
Chapter 13: The Fundamentals Of Rider Safety A Parents' Guide	83
Chapter 14: Health – What Does That Actually Mean?	108
Chapter 15: The Biochemistry Of Healing	112
Chapter 16: Muscle Health	122

Chapter 17: What About The Horse? Common Injuries After A Fall	131
Chapter 18: Wound Repair And Tissue Healing Hacks	135
Chapter 19: The Foundations Of Rider Fitness, Balance And Biomechanics	137
Chapter 20: Smart Recovery – How To Use Neuroscience And Cell Biology To Reduce Recovery Times	150
Chapter 21: Balance And The Brain – The Science Of Learning And Adaptation	154
Chapter 22: Brain-Retraining: Foundational Balance Exercise Homework	161
Chapter 23: A Sneak Peak – How To Recover Quickly And Effectively	166
Chapter 24: Our Falls Prevention UK Survey	177
Chapter 25: Feedback And Advice From The Professionals	182
Chapter 26: A Few Big Thank Yous	185
Chapter 27: References For Further Reading	190
Chapter 28: How To Get In Touch For A Consultation	194

CHAPTER 1
INTRODUCTION

As a passionate horse rider and advocate for equestrian safety, I am excited to present this book dedicated to equipping fellow riders with essential knowledge and strategies to help prevent long-term issues occurring after a fall. Having experienced the exhilaration and challenges of riding firsthand, I understand the inherent risks associated with this beloved sport. However, with proper education and proactive measures, the likelihood of sustaining severe injuries can be significantly reduced, resulting in a safer riding experience for all.

This book aims to address a critical aspect of horse riding safety: preventing long-term injuries after a fall. While falls are an inevitable part of equestrian pursuits, the aftermath can often extend beyond immediate physical injuries, potentially impacting our long-term well-being and enjoyment of riding. By implementing practical techniques and fostering a safety-first mindset, riders can better protect themselves and minimise the risk of enduring lasting harm.

Through this book, I endeavour to provide comprehensive insights, practical tips and actionable strategies tailored to riders of all levels. Whether you're a seasoned equestrian or just starting your riding journey, the information presented in this book will empower you to ride confidently, mitigate risks and safeguard your long-term health and vitality. Together, let's embark on this journey towards safer, more enjoyable horse-riding experiences.

MEET THE AUTHOR

In March 2024, following yet another fall from my esteemed warmblood, Blue, I made the decision to embark on writing this book. Standing at an imposing 18.1hh, Blue possesses a commanding presence, albeit with the occasional challenge in consistent teamwork, a characteristic of many warmbloods. His spirited nature occasionally introduces unexpected elements into our training sessions. Our usual

pursuits involve competitive engagements within the UK's British Showjumping (BS), British Dressage (BD) and low-level arena eventing circuits.

I managed to come to the second part of a dog-leg to a full up 1.10m oxer and interfered (unintentionally) with the canter rhythm, thus throwing the horse off his stride. So, he made the decision to abruptly stop, and I tumbled over his left shoulder, landing in the fence and wings. Ouch! Now my sacroiliac joints are both fixed solid and my L5 vertebra has an extension injury causing nerve inflammation. My road to recovery has been shared with you at the end of the book if you are interested.

Reflecting on my 35 years of equestrian experience, I acknowledge that the overwhelming majority of falls I've encountered have been attributable to rider error, occurring particularly during high-speed jumping practice. This realisation underscores the critical importance of enhancing rider skills and safety practices, prompting me to compile this book as an easy-to-understand resource for fellow equestrians seeking to minimise risks and maximise safety in their riding endeavours.

My extensive educational background as a fully qualified human and animal Chiropractor, coupled with my memberships in prestigious professional associations such as the Royal College of Chiropractors Specialist Animal Faculty, the British Chiropractic Association, and the British Animal Chiropractic Association, make me an ideal candidate to write this book on horse riding safety.

My qualifications and affiliations demonstrate my deep understanding of human and animal biomechanics, anatomy, and musculoskeletal health, all of which are

critical aspects of equestrian safety. My expertise in chiropractic care equips me with valuable insights into injury prevention and rehabilitation, as well as holistic approaches to wellness, directly applicable to horse riders' safety and well-being.

Furthermore, my involvement in organisations such as RAMP, the International Veterinary Chiropractic Association and the International Association of Veterinary Rehabilitation and Physical Therapists highlights my commitment to staying abreast of the latest advancements and best practices in animal healthcare and rehabilitation. This expertise enables me to provide evidence-based recommendations and strategies tailored to mitigate the risks of long-term injuries for horse riders.

Furthermore, my additional expertise in paediatric specialisms, sports injuries and psychology, and brain neurodevelopmental integration and primitive reflexes further enhance my ability to address the complex interplay between physical and psychological factors impacting rider safety.

In summary, my diverse educational background and professional affiliations uniquely position me to author a book that combines practical insights, scientific knowledge and expert guidance to empower equestrians to ride safely and prevent long-term injuries.

UNDERSTANDING EQUESTRIAN SAFETY

The prevalence of falls from horses is of significant concern, with recent studies revealing a considerable percentage of riders experience falls. Notably, the frequency of accidents tends to rise during the darker months, possibly due to reduced visibility. Surprisingly, equestrian activities have been identified as presenting a higher hospital admission rate than many other high-risk sports, emphasizing the importance of protective gear, which, regrettably, is not consistently utilised. The statistics provoke a reflection on the unreported injuries within the equestrian community and highlight the necessity for enhanced protective measures and educational campaigns focused on preventing rider injuries.

CHAPTER 2
HORSE RIDING SAFETY

HOW COMMON IS IT TO FALL OFF A HORSE?

According to the most recent worldwide research published by the World Health Organization (2021) and the Brain Injury Association (2023), half of all riders have fallen off at least once. A fall was defined as contact with the ground. The latest British Equestrian survey (2023) also showed that 84% of riders have fallen off at least once, and half of the riders surveyed had fallen two or more times.

According to the American national safety council 81% of riders will experience an injury at some point, and 21% of those will be a serious injury. Considering there are around three million known equestrians in the USA, then that is an alarming number of injuries.

Apparently, accidents occur more often in the darker months, between October and December. This is possibly due to road user visibility, but the research is unclear.

In 2023 the FEI eventing committee chair highlighted the need for all disciplines to start tracking falls, since from 2018 until present day "25% of total falls recorded, did not happen at cross-country fences". The only way we will learn more about this is therefore to start tracking the number of falls and also the outcomes.

According to Statista, the US Government's global data and business intelligence platform, a study of 45,671 people with equestrian injuries who had visited a hospital was conducted in 2018. The study found the dangers of equestrian activities have been "severely under-appreciated". When the activity was carried out for hours at a time, horse riding resulted in a "higher proportion of hospital admission than other higher risk activities like skiing".

We all know that protective gear can save lives, but unfortunately it is not always worn. Studies have shown that a large fraction of riders involved in equestrian injuries were not wearing helmets at the time of their accident. "It stands to reason that raising awareness of the possible injuries and increasing preventive measures to protect against head injuries would significantly reduce mortality" (National Trauma Data Bank 2023, CDC 2021). Interestingly, hospital "admission risk from horse riding is higher than football, auto and motorcycle racing, and skiing" (Journal of Trauma Management and Outcomes, 2006). Recently, some attention has been paid by equestrian sporting agencies to the use of protective equipment to prevent injuries, especially as it relates to concussion and brain injuries. However, very few public health campaigns have focused on preventing injuries related to riders using horses for leisure and work.

My concerns about many of these reported statistics lies in the fact that among the 30 million equestrians currently riding in the US, a significant portion may have experienced injuries that they themselves deemed insufficiently severe enough to warrant a hospital visit. I

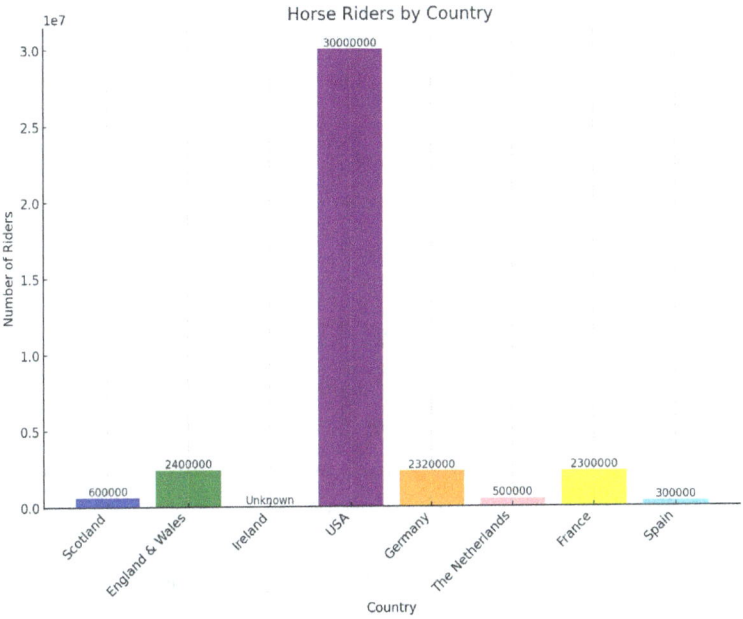

Source: Statista Research Department UK (2023).

ponder how the statistics would appear if every injury, regardless of perceived severity, were accurately reported.

https://www.bmj.com/company/newsroom/serious-injury-risk-higher-for-horse-riding-than-for-football-motor-racing-or-skiing/

According to the British Horse Industry Confederation and Department for Environment, Food and Rural Affairs (DEFRA), 2.4 million people ride in England and Wales and around 600k in Scotland and Ireland.

http://www.defra.gov.uk/rural/horses/topics/research.htm

According to the British Horse Society, 50% of UK horse rider accidents occur on the roads. In 2022, the

Fédération Equestre Internationale (FEI) reported that 25% of reported falls during their events, did not happen at cross-country fences as assumed, but on the flat. This means that ideally all other disciplines should be recording falls data on a regular basis and submitting them to a central database.

SURELY ONLY GREEN RIDERS FALL OFF?

No! The misconception that only novice riders experience falls is inaccurate. Research indicates that professional equestrians encounter more severe accidents, albeit less frequently, typically due to the complexities and heightened difficulty levels of their activities.

Consequently, riders with extensive experience are at a higher risk of sustaining injuries. Moreover, professional riders often handle multiple horses daily, which may

belong to other owners and possess varying degrees of training and predictability. Adapting to each horse's unique movement patterns, balance, gait and temperament demands considerable skill and proficiency. Additionally, the physical demands of riding, coupled with daily stable duties, pose further risks for injuries, including repetitive strain injuries that can accumulate over time.

The top five most common reasons for falling

1) Sudden changes in direction from the horse, unseating the rider.
2) Defective or unsuitable equipment. Saddles slipping or reins breaking etc.
3) An unsuitable horse: incorrectly matched pairs will have more mistakes and inexperienced riders may not be able to correct issues that can lead to accidents.
4) Poor surface: horses can stumble or slip on unfamiliar or slippery surfaces.
5) Competitions and events: according to a Cambridge University (2002) study on spinal injuries resulting from horse riding injuries, in the study of 1000 riders, there was the equivalent of one injury for every five hours of cross-country eventing vs one injury for every 100 hours of leisure riding.

CHAPTER 3
FALL RECOVERY (IT TAKES A VILLAGE)

It's crucial to emphasise the urgency of seeking prompt medical attention after falling off a horse. Whether it's a casual hack, arena workout or competitive event, a seemingly harmless fall can quickly escalate into a serious injury or even a fatality (undiagnosed head injuries or neck fractures). While most falls result in minor bruises, the potential for severe harm is always present. Unlike other activities where safety protocols are taught and understood, such as swimming or gymnastics, the same level of preparedness is often lacking in equestrian pursuits. Given the unpredictable nature of riding and the sheer power of horses, it's imperative to prioritise fall safety and be prepared to address any potential injuries promptly.

Unfortunately, not all riders wear safety gear on a regular basis either, which means the potential for risk is much higher than in other sports.

Your best chance of a positive long-term recovery is to seek a team of experts that understand exactly what is required to get you an accurate diagnosis, design a specific treatment plan to achieve your goals and then actually have the knowledge, skills and expertise to deliver those results.

For example, at Riverside Chiropractic Group, many of our equestrian patients have chosen to work with us on their recoveries because of our focus on their long-term success. We understand that your body should be able to consistently function at the optimum level, which then helps elevate your immune system to enhance your overall health and well-being, and therefore reduce your chances of long-term disease processes taking hold.

Each person's journey should be different, as each person's goals, background and medical histories are unique.

Clinical Tip: If anyone is giving you a set of generic stretches on a handout – find a new team to work with!

We don't believe in lazy healthcare where generic stretches and exercise plans are appropriate to the entire cohort.

Exercise should be tailor made and dynamic, adapting as your body changes and becomes more resilient.

LISA'S STORY (2021)

"I chose Riverside Chiropractic Group because everything was under one roof. Emma had been recommended to me by a friend and I had seen so many other people who couldn't help me. I was at my wits' end and nearly gave up riding completely. Thankfully, I took a chance and booked in with Emma. I thought that Chiropractors were all about cracking backs, but boy was I wrong. She spent the time finding out about how my life had changed since Misty, my Connemara Misty, had fallen on top of me. I was out hacking and slipped in a ditch when a driver came too close, and he got a fright. The result – my pelvis was shattered, and I now have pins in my right leg. Although I certainly didn't feel like the bionic woman at the time.

I was utterly devastated that this had happened to me. Once I was patched up, I felt that I was then pushed away and left to my own devices. I tried physical therapy, but the exercises were so painful that I couldn't do at least 80% of them. The practitioner didn't seem concerned and would just tell me to come back in a month. I was getting really depressed as my horses live at home, and mucking out and usual yard duties were becoming unbearable. Normally I loved hacking alone and never felt worried about my safety. But now, the chore of just getting the ponies in and out every day made my body groan with every step.

I remember going to see a private physiotherapist who told me to download an app about mindfulness, enjoy the sunshine and be grateful for what I have. I was so upset that when I left, I broke down and cried in the car for 30 minutes. I have two young children, four ponies and a menagerie of animals to look after, as well as a husband and a full-time job. Was this really as good as it would ever get? Did no one care that I wanted to get better?

My goals were never even discussed until I met Emma and her team at RCG. It was a revelation to have someone really listen, who was a rider themselves and who actually gave a crap about what I wanted and needed for a change. This time my tears flowed from relief and joy that someone was happy to work with me to get stronger again. The road to success is never easy, but getting back on my boy again and being able to play with my kids like a regular mum has been the real icing on the cake. I feel more empowered than ever and was happy to share my success story with you today." Lisa, 41, Aberdeenshire.

WHAT DID LISA'S STORY TEACH US?

Lisa taught me a valuable lesson about the importance of training all medical practitioners to shut up and really listen. Unfortunately, her story is heard too frequently in clinical practice these days, and it reminds me why I chose to work in healthcare in the first place. To actually help people! I'm sure in hindsight, or rather I'm hopeful, if this professional had really listened to Lisa's story, their advice would have been more supportive and more effective. But in this instance, it was ill timed, illogical and without empathy. Lisa is happy for us to share her story as her life has changed dramatically since this day, and she is stronger and happier than ever. She is even back doing local riding club events with her favourite Connemara companion.

Our mission and purpose changed the day I met Lisa. We knew that, sadly, personal healthcare was nearly extinct in the UK system, so we made it our number one goal to bring back quality, personal healthcare for the entire family. To provide long-term preventative care and full body wellness.

The five keys hacks for successful recovery

- Pain Reduction – Find an expert with different treatment techniques and effective options to suit your health history.
- Increase Your Movement – Find an expert with knowledge of how to reduce stiffness and restrictions common in your particular sport. Thus, increasing mobility in your entire body and allowing you the freedom again to have better control and performance.
- Understanding Your Problem – You will need someone who truly understands exactly what's causing your problem. Only then will you learn how to prevent future issues.
- Get Back to Doing What You Love – Whether it's riding, running, yoga, weight training or just sitting comfortably. Get help to resolve all your limiting issues from head to toe.
- Save Time – Seeking professional advice and treatment can save you weeks, months or even years trying different remedies to treat the underlying

cause of your problem. Get results now, by choosing an expert who is qualified to get you on the road to recovery and who can see it all the way through to success!

Clinical Tip: No matter what direction you choose in terms of medical experts, just get checked. ☑

Scan the QR Code when you want to visit us in person or book a virtual consultation from the comfort of your home.

Our Clinical Locations:
- Riverside Chiropractic Clinic, 581-585 Holburn Street, Aberdeen, Scotland, UK
- Westhill Business Centre, Aberdeenshire
- Aberdeenshire Chiropractic Clinic, Oldmeldrum

Book now

CHAPTER 4
THE TRUTH ABOUT CONCUSSION

Concussion is a frequently under diagnosed condition which is important to recognise and manage appropriately. While diagnosis needs to be confirmed by a healthcare professional, you can learn tips on how to recognise it here.

Concussion can present in a variety of ways and will differ from person to person. Signs and symptoms can be physical, cognitive or behavioural, and it's important to remember that they can take hours or sometimes days to appear.

WHAT SHOULD I DO IF I SUSPECT A CONCUSSION?

If you believe you or someone else has suffered a concussion following a fall from a horse, or a blow to the head, face, neck or body, take immediate action. The person must

immediately cease all ridden, equestrian-related activity and any potentially strenuous mental or physical activity, then you should follow the four Rs...

- Recognise the signs and symptoms
- Remove the injured person from the scene
- Recover until all symptoms have been resolved
- Return gradually to activity

Each rider should be advised to rest for at least 48 hours after a concussion. This allows your delayed onset muscle soreness, whiplash or brain rattle to have a chance to settle and begin to recover.

At which point, I advise you to have a neurological exam with your health specialist. We offer neurological testing on all our horse riders post-fall, to assess them for signs of post-concussion injury, cognitive impairment or balance disorders that can manifest 72 hours later.

Horse riding is not advised until seven days post-concussion, as it has high risks associated with head impact and increased cardiovascular intensity and fragility. Proper training, sport-specific exercises and running are not to be performed until 14 days post-concussion. Return to regular exercise no sooner than three weeks after any concussion.

Clinical Tip: If in doubt, your healthcare professional can utilise the sport concussion assessment tool called SCAT6 to evaluate your concussion (age 13+).
https://bjsm.bmj.com/content/bjsports/51/11/851.full.pdf

WHEN TO SEEK IMMEDIATE MEDICAL ATTENTION AFTER SOMEONE FALLS

If the person is unconscious, call an ambulance. Do not attempt to move them or remove their riding hat due to the risk of spinal cord injuries. The only exception to this is if they are having difficulty breathing, in which case get them into the recovery position.

▶ **Red flags are symptoms that require investigation ASAP:**
- Neck pain
- Severe or worsening headache
- Weakness or tingling in the limbs
- Vomiting
- Double vision
- Restless, agitated behaviour (out of character)
- Seizures or convulsions

🚦 **If the person who has fallen doesn't have any red flags (but isn't quite right):**
- Do not let them get back on their horse
- Don't let them drive home by themselves

- Don't let them leave the venue without someone checking them over, ask them to walk in a straight line or on a virtual tight rope
- Ask them a couple of memory questions to check they are lucid and capable (who were you riding with? What day is it? What have you got planned next with your horse?)
- Contact their nominated emergency contact person and speak to them directly to get an appointment arranged asap with a medical professional
- Ask them to refrain from any physical activity for 48 hours
- Advise them to refrain from any device use/reading/TV/gaming for 48 hours
- They shouldn't be left alone for the first couple of hours when they return home
- No alcohol or sleeping tablets for the first 24 hours
- No driving until cleared by a medical professional

Clinical Tip: Do not return to sport or any exercise without being cleared by a medical professional who has advanced neurological assessment training.

CHAPTER 5

UNDERSTANDING AND RECOVERING FROM WHIPLASH FOR HORSE RIDERS

WHAT IS WHIPLASH?

Whiplash is a neck injury resulting from forceful, rapid back-and-forth movement of the neck, akin to the cracking of a whip. This type of injury is common in falls, especially for horse riders who might experience

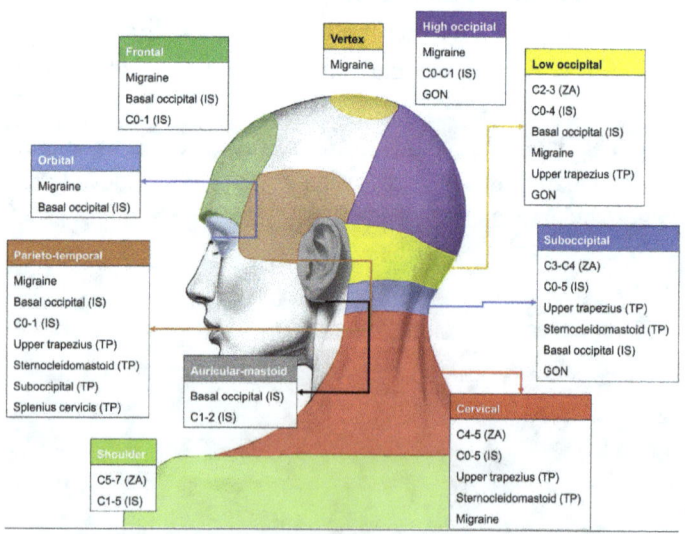

The image above shows the various regions of the head and neck and the common reasons for pain in each section.

sudden stops, collisions or falls from their mounts. Whiplash primarily affects the soft tissues of the neck, including the muscles, ligaments and tendons, potentially leading to a range of physical ailments.

SYMPTOMS OF WHIPLASH

The symptoms of whiplash can vary widely in severity and duration but typically include:

- Neck pain and stiffness
- Headaches – often starting at the base of the skull
- Dizziness
- Blurred vision
- Fatigue
- Irritability
- Difficulty concentrating
- Memory problems
- Tinnitus (ringing in the ears)
- Sleep disturbance
- Depression

It's crucial for horse riders to recognise these symptoms early to manage the condition effectively and prevent further injury.

HOW LONG WILL IT LAST?

The duration of whiplash symptoms can significantly vary from one individual to another. While some may recover within a few weeks, others may experience symptoms for several months or even longer. Factors that can influence the duration of symptoms include the severity of the initial injury, the immediate response to the injury, and the overall health and age of the individual. This is why prompt and appropriate treatment is key to a speedy recovery.

BEST TREATMENT AND WHY

Treatment for whiplash typically involves a combination of rest, pain management and physical hands-on therapies like manipulation to the cervical and thoracic spine, soft tissue work on ligaments, massage, sports taping, laser therapy, acupuncture and rehab exercises.

The body and nervous system needs a system reset or reboot to discard the feedback messages into the spinal cord and brain of "injury or damage" to allow successful initiation of the healing process. These therapies have proven success and can be used safely in the hands of an expert.

REST AND PAIN MANAGEMENT

In the immediate aftermath of the injury, short-term rest and pain management through over-the-counter pain relievers or prescribed medications can help reduce inflammation and manage pain.

Although many experts believe that NSAIDs like ibuprofen can reduce the bodies naturally capacity for healing so I would suggest a topical (gel/cream) formula onto affected areas like your neck and shoulders. Heat/ice can also be very helpful to reduce initial pain. Although the medical communities opinions and the research is conflicting on which is best. Most agree that an application of either heat/ice should be for 15 minutes 3 x daily for the first 3-5 days.

> **Clinical Tip:** Prolonged inactivity is discouraged as it can delay recovery.

HOW QUICKLY SHOULD I BEGIN PHYSICAL THERAPY?

As soon as possible, engaging in physical therapy is crucial. A qualified therapist can provide targeted exercises to restore range of motion, strengthen the muscles around the neck and improve posture. This active approach helps speed up recovery and can reduce the risk of chronic symptoms.

Understanding proper posture and ergonomics, especially while riding, can prevent further neck strain. Professional guidance on safe riding and fall techniques can also mitigate the risk of re-injury.

WHEN TO SEEK PROFESSIONAL ADVICE

While mild symptoms of whiplash can often be managed with home care, there are several circumstances under which it's crucial to seek professional medical advice:

- Symptoms persist or worsen over time
- Severe neck pain or headaches
- Pain that spreads to the shoulders or arms
- Numbness, weakness or tingling in the arms
- Difficulty with balance or coordination
- Any signs of concussion, such as memory loss or confusion
- Immediately or within 48 hours if possible

For horse riders, a professional evaluation is also recommended to assess when it's safe to return to riding and to receive tailored advice on preventing future injuries.

In conclusion, whiplash is a common but manageable condition for horse riders, with prompt and appropriate treatment playing a crucial role in recovery. Understanding the symptoms, treatment options and when to seek professional advice can empower riders to manage their recovery effectively and return to their passion with confidence.

CHAPTER 6
CHILDREN AND FALLS – RISKS AND REWARDS

Horse riding is a wonderful sport and brings joy to the millions of riders and spectators worldwide who enjoy the exhilaration of having a true connection and bond with an animal. Horses are more than pets; they show a multitude of deep emotions and more empathy than many humans.

Top Five Benefits of horse riding for children

Horse riding offers a variety of benefits for children, particularly in developing strength, balance, and other key skills. Here are the top five benefits:

- **Physical Fitness and Core Strength:** Riding a horse requires the rider to engage and stabilise their core muscles to maintain balance on the horse. This continuous adjustment and balance improves core strength, crucial for overall body strength and stability.
- **Balance and Coordination:** Horse riding is an excellent exercise for developing balance. As the horse moves, the rider must constantly adjust their posture to stay balanced, which enhances their

ability to coordinate their movements effectively with the horse.
- **Motor Skills Development:** The act of controlling a horse requires a combination of fine and gross motor skills. Riders learn to use delicate hand movements to guide the horse, along with larger leg and body movements to maintain their position. This helps to refine both types of motor skills.
- **Posture Improvement:** Good posture is essential in horse riding. Riders learn to sit up straight and hold their head up while riding, which translates into better posture in daily activities. The strength gained in the back and shoulders from riding supports this improved posture. Grooming and mucking out also develop mid back postural muscles. A set of safety steps can be very useful for grooming to reduce neck strain.
- **Sensory Integration:** Horse riding offers a rich sensory experience that can help children with sensory integration issues. The movement of the horse provides vestibular stimulation (sense of balance), while the need to adjust to the horse's movements offers proprioceptive inputs (sense of body position). This can be particularly beneficial for children with sensory processing disorders.

Beyond these physical benefits, horse riding also contributes to emotional and social development, such as building confidence, fostering a sense of responsibility and encouraging empathy and communication. It's a multifaceted activity that supports a child's growth in numerous ways.

SHOULD MY CHILD BE CHECKED AFTER A FALL?

Absolutely! In daily clinical practice we help riders of all ages, particularly after falls and accidents. We improve their healing times, body mechanics and balance through manual therapy and rehabilitation.

In the last ten years, the number of children being brought in to our clinic for sport-related accidents has tripled. In particular, we deem horse riding specific falls among children being grossly disproportionately underestimated. We often hear the phrase "children just bounce" which as you now know, just isn't true at all.

Generally, children under 14 do recover faster, as their body's ability to heal is proportionally quicker due to:

- Rapid cell growth
- Stronger immune systems
- More elasticity in their collagen
- Less fascial adhesions
- Lack of fear avoidance behaviours
- Adequate hydration

However, this does not mean they should not be checked regularly by an expert. Especially after a fall, children should ideally be assessed within 72 hours.

They should not be able to return to sport or activity until they have been checked by a medical professional, who understands biomechanics, neurology and brain trauma and tissue recovery.

Clinical Tip: Do not underestimate the need for a checkup after a fall! Long-term smaller issues could compound and lead to potentially serious outcomes.

We must avoid young, developing bodies integrating negative movement patterns and reduced hazard awareness and proprioceptive awareness.

Many adult riders describe a particular fall in childhood which they believe was the "start of all their back problems".

Horse riding is a very athletic sport. Therefore, children should be taught how to think like an athlete. Prepare, execute, optimise, learn, recovery, retrain.

If in doubt, take your child to a biomechanics expert like a CHIROPRACTOR or qualified PHYSIOTHERAPIST to get a proper check up with a team of experts who specialise in treating children.

> Clinical Tip: Many musculoskeletal injuries can take up to 12 weeks to fully repair. This process can be completed quicker through an accurate diagnosis, a tailor-made treatment plan, laser therapy and suitable rehabilitation.

Treatment should always be adapted specifically to meet children's needs; their body mechanics are different to adults. Also, each child's treatment type and choices including consent, are paramount. At our clinics, we always make sure each child has a very positive experience with healthcare providers where they can ask questions and receive appropriate answers.

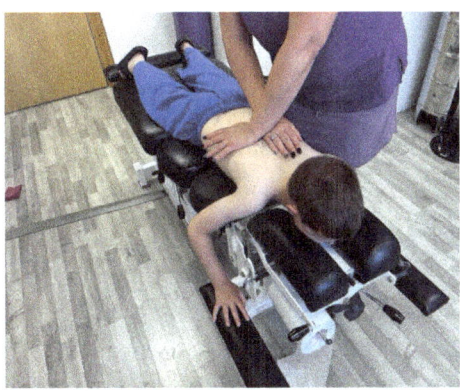

Negative experiences with healthcare professionals at a young age can lead to the avoidance of seeking care later as an adult. It is vital that the right person is selected to see your child.

Children under 16 must always be accompanied by a parent/guardian, as consent will need to be provided by both parties.

For healthcare professionals use only

Children's concussion form for medical professional use. (Ages 5-12 year olds) https://bjsm.bmj.com/content/bjsports/early/2017/04/28/bjsports-2017-097492childscat5.full.pdf

> Clinical Tip: If a child is complaining about pain, listen to them. They have exactly the same number of pain receptors in their bodies as you do! They may not have the tools to articulate the amount of pain that they are experiencing, especially if it's their first real injury.
>
> I always remind parents that if they can point to the location, and it's the same place every time, then there's certainly an issue to be investigated and most likely treated.

ENSURING YOUR CHILD'S SAFETY IN EQUESTRIAN SPORTS: ESSENTIAL GEAR FOR YOUNG RIDERS

Embarking on the journey of equestrian sports with your child is an exhilarating experience filled with both excitement and responsibility. The paramount concern for any parent or guardian should be the safety and preparedness of their young rider. A critical step in this preparation is equipping them with the essential safety gear that can significantly reduce the risk of injury.

The Foundation of Safety: A Well-Fitted Riding Hat

At the forefront of necessary equipment is a well-fitted riding hat. The significance of this piece cannot be overstated; it serves as the primary line of defence against head injuries. Opting for a jockey skull cap is particularly advisable. Its design allows for cover changes, accommodating the evolving fashion trends in the equestrian world without compromising on safety. This adaptability ensures that your child remains both protected and stylish.

The Non-Negotiable: Body Protectors

Another indispensable item of safety gear is the body protector. I cannot stress enough the importance of all children donning these protectors at all times during horse riding activities, irrespective of their skill level. The equestrian realm, while rewarding, harbours risks of falls and impacts that can lead to severe, long-term health complications. My extensive experience treating riders over the past 15 years has revealed a stark reality: many enduring health issues stem from injuries that could have been mitigated, or even prevented, with adequate body protection.

Optimal Protection: The Combination of Semi-Rigid Frames and Air Jackets

For ultimate safeguarding, I advocate for a combination of a semi-rigid frame body protector, specifically tailored for the young equestrian athlete, and an air jacket. This duo offers a robust shield against the unpredictable nature of horse riding. The semi-rigid frame provides consistent protection, while the air jacket offers additional impact absorption in the event of a fall.

Comprehensive Head and Neck Safety

The emphasis on head protection extends beyond riding; children should also wear their riding hats while grooming and leading horses. The unpredictable behaviour of horses, coupled with their physical advantage, poses a significant risk. The substantial difference in skull thickness and

size between a child and a horse underscores the critical need for constant head and neck protection, especially considering the developing brains of young riders.

Embarking on a Safe Equestrian Journey
As we guide our children through the enriching path of equestrian sports, their safety should always be our guiding light. Equipping them with the right safety gear is not just a precaution, it's a necessity. By ensuring our young riders are well-protected, we foster an environment where they can confidently explore, learn and grow in the sport they love, all while minimising the risks that accompany it.

CHAPTER 7
SAFETY STANDARDS: BEST PRACTICE AND THE LAW

Some key facts about horse riding, injuries and the law:

- 74.83% of equestrian deaths are caused by head and neck injuries
- Thoracic injuries were the second highest cause of death with 18.44%
- Abdominal injuries caused the third highest number of deaths with 5.31%
- UK safety standards are found on the governing bodies' websites and should be checked regularly as rules are amended in line with new manufacturing guidelines and perform standards.
- In the UK, the Health and Safety Executive (HSE) requires all accidents to be reported to the RIDDOR reporting website that involve loss of consciousness caused by a head injury, fractures (except for fingers and toes) and any crush injury to the torso or head

HATS AND HELMETS

Wearing a riding hat reduces the risk of severe head injury by 50%, which is not much when you think about it. But it reduces the risk of severe brain injury by 85%.

Why? Our brain is still moving while we hit the ground, increasing the chance of further injury occurring. A bit like shaking a snow globe where the water takes time to settle again after being shaken. In actual fact or brain tissue itself does not compress like a sponge under force in the linear plane and is unable to withstand rotational shear forces (like spinning a carousel at the fair).

> **Clinical Tip:** Impacts from falls are often forward and vertical velocity. This means that helmets need to withstand motion in all directions. It's actually the rotational strains that cause concussions to riders.
>
> Wearing a well fitted, properly fastened protective headgear is absolutely essential to mitigate the risk of serious head injury and/or concussion in case of a fall. The FEI urges all equestrian athletes to wear protective headgear whenever riding a horse or driving a carriage.

NEW HAT STANDARDS AND THE FUTURE OF HELMETS

Rotational velocity is how quickly an object rotates relative to a point. In the context of a rider, it's similar to the end of a whip. When a whip cracks, it is because the loop at the end accelerates with rotational velocity until it creates a sonic boom. A rider's body is like the length of the whip, and the head is like the loop at the end.

They have found in recent studies that rotational forces on the brain seem to be "significantly" reduced in sand and sand plus fibre surfaces.

Research is currently underway on how hats themselves could potentially absorb more rotational forces on impact. This is through the use of the MIPS system. However, at this time, the main issue is designing a hat that can mitigate the speed required to move the hat at peak loading capacity before the brain receives the forces.

HOW OFTEN SHOULD YOUR HAT BE CHANGED?

Every two to three years! Even if your riding hat hasn't endured any impact, it's essential to replace it regularly. Over time, the protective materials within the hat deteriorate due to exposure to heat and continuous use, diminishing its protective capabilities. For daily riders, it's actually recommended to replace the helmet annually, while occasional riders should do so every two to three years. Always replace your hat after a fall to ensure continued safety. If you suspect any damage to your hat, err on the side of caution and replace it without delay, as head safety should never be compromised.

It is strongly recommended you replace your riding hat **immediately** if you have suffered a fall and the hat has taken impact. If you have dropped it, if there are any dents, or if there is fraying to the lining or straps, it may not serve its purpose anymore and you should replace it.

Don't be tempted to sell your worn hat, either. Doing so could jeopardise the safety of the rider that buys it from you. Make sure you always buy your hat from a reputable source and don't buy second hand. Hats should always be fitted by a qualified hat fitting centre. Remember, your insurance may depend on it.

Wow! Literally while compiling this book, a new brand in equestrian blend design has just unveiled its newest product. "Evoke has announced the launch of a helmet replacement policy. Should a rider suffer a fall within six months of buying and registering their Evoke helmet, the scheme guarantees to provide a replacement helmet with a 50% discount."

SAFETY STANDARDS AND THE LAW 2024

BETA STANDARDS POSTER: https://www.beta-uk.org/media.php

British BETA Guide to body protectors: https://www.beta-uk.org/media.php

AVOIDABLE CAUSES OF INJURY

A 2018 research report on horse riding injuries statistics found that the majority of horse riding injuries could have been prevented and injuries were due to rider or handler errors.

#1 Avoidable Cause   Broken/damaged tack
#2 Avoidable Cause   Slipped saddle
#3 Avoidable Cause   No safety checks before setting off (head and body protection, mobile phone, informing others of your location/ intentions)

This study analysed horse riding accidents and injuries and found that 66% of injuries were actually preventable. Great news!

CHAPTER 8
HOW TO PREPARE FOR FALLS

Prepare yourself for the inevitability of falling or needing to dismount from your horse by adopting proactive measures. Begin by learning how to fall and roll away safely. Practise on soft ground like a sandy arena while wearing standard riding attire and a riding hat. Have a friend observe the exercise and record it on your phone for you to review later.

> **Clinical Tip:** Practice helps turn movement patterns into a learnt behaviour and a response called neural plasticity. In other words, your brain will be able to recall that specific movement faster using muscle memory.

SHOULD I PRACTISE FALLING?

According to the stunt people…you can practise falls safety by initially wearing a hard hat and body protector and using either a crash mat, your mattress at home or a well maintained, clean surfaced arena to practise.

Make sure the area around you is safe and completely clear of debris and potential obstacles before attempting

any practice. Also make sure that a responsible adult is around to supervise and mitigate risks. Stunt people use back braces similar to this one to protect their spines during practice. They also wear shoulder and knee pads, elbow pads and wrist straps.

This is a representation of what I have been wearing for horse riding for the last five years, even to daily basic training. I am not affiliated with any of these products.

Charles Owen has recently designed an equestrian product called "The shadow" which is a back protector similar to these motor cross protectors for riders who would like a breathable daily use alternative.

They also have a body protector suitable for all equestrian events called the Kontour. This has been recommended by many UK retailers as one of their customer's favourites as the length of the product can be somewhat altered to fit more accurately due to the shoulder straps.

The other equestrian product that has been a big hit in the UK is the new brand, FOMO, designed by a rider and Sports Engineer. This protector has particularly high popularity for its comfort in all weather conditions.

However, please bear in mind that if you choose to use anything out with our industry that the equipment designed for equestrians purposely has a much more rigid design, which is much more likely to help to prevent "crush injuries" around your rib cage and internal organs, should the horse land on you. Therefore, they are much better suited to equestrian pursuits than the ones shown above. Although compared to wearing nothing at all, at least these options are breathable and easy to move in.

In terms of future developmental designs, I would encourage equestrian companies to design a daily use version like the ones above, which would also incorporate a semi-rigid rib cage frame built into it. I would also support decisions for every body protector to have shoulder protection and a longer frame for pelvic protection. Ideally there would be a range of lengths available to suit the variety of equestrian rider heights.

I would suggest that an underwear top version be designed that would incorporate the elbow and shoulder pads that can help prevent many superficial sprains and strains, including clavicle and elbow fractures which are debilitating especially for anyone who has their horses at home.

CLINICAL TIP: There is some excellent gear available for stunt riders, BMX, skiing, rugby and snowboarding. However, they are not equestrian safety standard specific. Remember you can only wear British Standard equestrian specific body protectors for competitions, which is compulsory.

The protective gear donned by mountain bikers often surpasses what we typically wear in equestrian activities in terms of safety. Considering the similarities in speed and terrain, it prompts a thought-provoking question: Should we in the equestrian community not borrow a page from their book? In other words, wear protective back and spinal safety equipment every time we ride – I would say absolutely!

The current approach towards protective gear in equestrian sports appears somewhat lax, especially when considering the need to safeguard areas frequently subjected to injury such as shoulders, backs, necks, wrists, pelvis and hips. The answer, quite evidently, is a resounding yes.

Imagine equestrian attire engineered with integrated spine and pelvis protection, complete with shoulder and elbow pads, as well as a rib and chest impact-absorbing framework. This would not just be protective gear, but akin to wearing shapewear designed for superheroes – merging aesthetics with unparalleled safety.

While various products in other sporting domains exist that are lightweight and breathable, they often fall short when it comes to providing adequate crush protection for the ribcage, unlike traditional equestrian body protectors.

The evolution of air jacket technology in recent times is noteworthy, yet it's disconcerting that only a single model currently offers neck protection. A glaring oversight in these designs is their lack of protection for the sacroiliac and hip joints, essential areas vulnerable during equestrian activities.

Current equestrian protectors, although effective to some degree, lack the daily usability, comfort and breathability needed in warmer climates. There lies a vast untapped potential to enhance equestrian safety gear through the integration of multi-sport technologies.

For instance, the longest spine protection gear I've discovered, designed for snowboarders by Cairn and named Pro Impackt D30, extends significant impact protection to the sacrum and spine. Yet, it leaves the hip joints exposed and unprotected. This gap highlights a critical area for development in equestrian safety technology.

> **Clinical Tip:** Obviously, the ground won't bounce like this in real life, but it's great to allow your body to get accustomed to the techniques. Trampoline parks are a great option for falls practice as they often they have large foam pits and larger spaces for you to practise on.

> **Clinical Tip:** Common sense rules should be applied here with regards to starting any practical exercises. Please do not even attempt these exercises if you are over 55, pregnant, have osteoporosis or EDS, are Vitamin D deficient or similar or are on anti-coagulant medications.

BOOTS AND FOOTWEAR

Unmounted boots are best to have a ridged sole, as mud and grassy terrains are slippery under foot. Wellingtons or muck boots made of rubber have limited foot arch support and should be avoided for equestrian purposes, as they can lead to back pain. Hard toe caps are recommended for instructors and yard staff – broken toes are common when handling horses.

Mounted footwear should be clean, well fitted and have an appropriate sole for stirrups. Toe stops for young inexperienced children are useful initially to stop their little feet sliding in the stirrups, but should be replaced with more appropriate sizes as the child develops their balance. Gloves are very important for protecting hands and as a precaution for rope burns. They also provide an improved grip and protect the delicate sensory nerve endings in our skin.

HOW TO FALL WITH STYLE

Apparently, jockeys and stunt riders begin by kneeling on one knee and turning their head and shoulders away from the direction of the "fall".

They then forward roll softly onto the mat/arena surface/mattress, and land smoothly on their mid back and not on the blade of their shoulder (which is more likely to fracture with impact). You should avoid impacting your neck and head directly by tucking your head in towards your chest with your chin down.

Draw your knees up and curl your arms to shield your head with your chin tucked towards your chest. Continue the motion onto your back and roll over onto your knees. Once on your knees, promptly rise to your feet. Repeat this exercise numerous times in both directions, dropping softly onto alternate knees to roll. Please note, if you have knee arthritis or cartilage damage or instability then this practice would be unsuitable.

> **Clinical Tip:** You are more likely to damage your neck and shoulders by trying to hold onto the reins. The horse is also more likely to panic if they go down and then feel restricted when trying to right themselves. They are flight prey animals, so their nervous system is hard-wired to respond to danger faster than ours is.

FOR THE STUNT RIDERS OUT THERE...

As you become more proficient, you could gradually increase the height of your controlled roll by standing on a small mounting block. While not every fall will mimic this scenario, practising these techniques provides a foundation for understanding fall mechanics.

WHY PRACTISE FOR FALLING?

The more fear we have about falling, the more apprehension we will have, which the horse will likely read and respond negatively to. The more worried we are, the more rigid we will move and then the more likely we will do some serious damage if we do fall again. It is critical that after the initial roll, you always aim to finish back up on your feet (where possible), enabling you to be more mobile and move away from any lingering danger like the jumps, obstacles or the horse itself.

IN SUMMARY

- Don't fall with your arms outstretched in front of you – that's how you could fracture your wrist

> **CLINICAL TIP:** Please bear in mind that every minor fall (even when intentional) can accumulate to a larger issue. Therefore, if you are planning on practising your falls, please visit your Chiropractor/physio before and after to avoid any compounding side effects.

- Try not to be rigid in your upper body as you fall – your end goal is to protect your head and neck
- Aim to land with your head tilted away from the ground as you fall, curling your body into a roll
- Martial artists will tell you to "relax into the fall", in other words, don't try to stop it from happening – that never works!
- Try to spread the impact onto larger surface areas like your bum, upper back or thighs where possible
- Don't get up straight away; adrenaline can play tricks letting you believe you are ok initially, and walking on a new fracture or dislocation can make things a lot worse.
- If your neck or head hurts straight away, stop and wait for someone to check you over

PREPARING MENTALLY FOR A FALL

Sometimes it feels like it all happens before you know what's hit you: usually the ground! However, on the occasions that you are jumping or doing poles or maybe have anticipated a quick spook or "monster", there is a brief moment of foresight when you can forward plan for possible outcomes.

When you sense an impending fall, it's crucial to grant yourself permission to let go. At that moment, redirect your focus towards separating yourself from the horse by kicking off the stirrups and releasing the reins. Clinging on can result in dangerous entanglement, being dragged at high speeds, getting kicked or trampled and sustaining fractures.

Allow your horse to roam freely; you can retrieve it later. As you begin to fall, aim to curl into a tight ball, tuck your chin to your chest, raise your arms in a protective stance with slightly bent elbows to shield your head and neck, and bring your knees close to your body.

Upon impact, roll away from the fall.

Preparing mentally for the inevitable falls in horse riding involves embracing a resilient mindset and practising mindfulness to enhance peripheral vision and overcome fear avoidance. Start by accepting that falls are a part of learning and growing in the sport, which can significantly reduce the anxiety associated with the possibility of falling.

Mental visualisation techniques are powerful: regularly visualise yourself riding confidently, including the scenario of a fall, and see yourself handling it in a safe and calm manner. This mental rehearsal not only prepares you for how to tuck and roll away, but also conditions your mind to react instinctively rather than with panic.

To enhance peripheral vision and situational awareness, practise exercises that require you to notice and react to peripheral stimuli, which can improve your ability to remain aware of your surroundings while focusing on riding. Exercises such as catching a ball from different angles while maintaining focus ahead can be beneficial. Incorporating mindfulness and meditation into your routine can help manage fear avoidance by grounding you in the present moment, enhancing focus and reducing anxiety. By training your mind to accept falls as part of the journey and to maintain awareness of your environment, you can build resilience, reduce fear and enhance your riding experience.

CHAPTER 9
THE PHYSICS BEHIND FALLING

Newton's second law of motion basically means that force equals mass multiplied by acceleration.

So…do not try to stop yourself falling by putting your arms out in front of you. The impact into your arms will be massive and because you cannot affect the speed (acceleration) or mass (your weight), then you need to protect your limbs by tucking them in to protect your head.

Some more physics about the horse… involving the law of inertia.

Newton's Laws

1. A body will remain at rest, or moving at a constant velocity, unless it is acted on by an unbalanced force.

2. The force experienced by an object is proportional to its mass times the acceleration it experiences:
$$\vec{F} = m\vec{a}$$

3. If two bodies exert a force on one another, the forces are equal in magnitude, but opposite in direction:
$$\vec{F}_{12} = -\vec{F}_{21}$$

When a horse suddenly stops while it is being ridden, a rider can be thrown forward and fall off the horse.

Why? When the horse is in motion, the rider is also in motion! When a horse abruptly stops, the lower part of the rider's body is stopped by the saddle, but the upper portion has no forces acting on it so the momentum will stay constant. As a result, the top half of the rider is thrown forward, causing the rider to be thrown off-balance and possibly fall off the horse.

WHAT EFFECT WILL A RIDER'S BODY MASS HAVE ON THE HORSE'S MECHANICS?

The thoracolumbar spine of a horse during ridden exercise is under additional forces due to the weight of the rider and saddle. A badly fitting saddles and pads can place additional pressure unevenly on the spine. This can cause pain and decrease function due to compensation patterns.

If the horse naturally has poor posture (croup high and large lordotic curved spine) then the pressures will be increased further. Changes in climate, shoeing and weight fluctuations have also been shown to affect muscle tone and size around the supporting regions of the spine and abdomen.

Incorporating Newton's laws of motion and the principles of biomechanics, the capacity of a horse to carry weight can be understood through a more scientific lens. According to the general consensus within equine biomechanics, a horse can comfortably support approximately 15-20% of its own body mass. This threshold is determined by analysing the distribution of forces acting on the horse's body, in alignment with Newton's second law of motion (Force = Mass x Acceleration). For example, a horse with a mass of 500 kilograms may be able bear a max load of up to 100 kilograms without significant trauma. This load encompasses both the rider's weight and the mass of any equipment such as saddles, bridles, heavy stirrup irons and training rugs.

Exceeding this load threshold could lead to adverse effects on the horse, aligning with Newton's third law of motion (for every action, there is an equal and opposite reaction). The additional force exerted on the horse's body by excessive weight can cause discomfort and lead to musculoskeletal strain, joint issues and even temporary lameness. Continuous overburdening may result in long-term damage. The horse's performance is also impacted; with increased mass, the force required for movement is greater, leading to quicker fatigue and a higher risk of stumbling and falls due to the compromised balance and mobility.

Observing the horse for signs of distress—such as laboured breathing, excessive sweating, elevated heart rate, lethargy and behavioural changes like dragging feet or showing tension in the neck and back—can serve as indicators of carrying too much weight. These signs suggest the horse is applying extra force to compensate for the excessive load, consistent with biomechanical principles.

The specific capacity of a horse to carry weight, whether closer to 15% or 20%, also depends on its breed, conditioning and overall health, reflecting the variable impact of forces on different bodies. The best method to assess a horse's comfort and capacity is through practical testing, while looking out for any signs of discomfort or strain as it moves.

For a practical application, an individual weighing 88 kilograms would require a horse with a mass between 500 to 666 kilograms to stay within the safe loading range, including the weight of the tack. This ensures the forces acting on the horse's body are within a manageable range, promoting well-being and performance according to the principles derived from Newton's laws and biomechanical analysis.

> **Clinical Tip:** According to orthopaedic surgeons "for every extra pound of weight that you have on your body, it's the same as eight extra pounds on your knee joints when weight bearing or exercising". (Dr Neilly, Aberdeen 2024)

GROUND REACTION FORCES

Newton's third law of motion: this is focused on, for example, when you jump, your legs apply a force to the ground, and the ground applies an equal and opposite reaction force that propels you into the air.

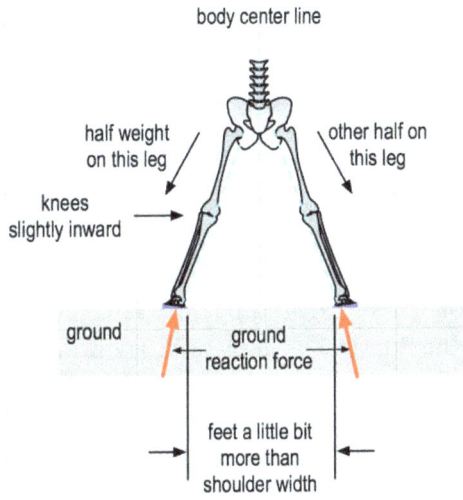

For the horse, ground reaction forces (GRFs) act in various directions and can be affected by the horse's body weight, gait, speed, shoeing and footing. This is why the "no foot; no horse" principle is so vital to normal horse function and wellness.

According to Hilary Clayton et al (2009), the weight of a rider affects the fore and hind limbs differently during locomotion.

GRFs are critical in understanding the interaction between an object, in this case, a horse, and the surface it moves on. These forces are the equal and opposite forces that the ground exerts on the horse as it moves, in accordance with Newton's third law of motion. Understanding GRFs is pivotal for several reasons, especially when analysing a horse's balance, strength and endurance, as they directly impact the biomechanical efficiency and overall health of the horse.

IMPACT ON BALANCE

Balance in horses, as in all moving bodies, is a dynamic process of maintaining stability through motion. GRFs are crucial in this context as they provide the necessary feedback for adjusting posture, stride and gait. When a horse's hoof strikes the ground, the GRF contributes to stabilising the horse by pushing back against the hoof with an equal force. Efficient use and absorption of these forces are essential for maintaining balance, particularly when performing complex manoeuvres that require significant changes in direction or speed. If a horse is unable to effectively manage these forces due to poor conformation, injury or fatigue, its balance will be compromised, leading to an increased risk of falls and injuries.

IMPACT ON STRENGTH

The adaptation of a horse's musculoskeletal system to GRFs can significantly influence its strength. Regular, controlled exposure to these forces through varied terrain and exercise can enhance musculoskeletal strength, much like resistance training in humans. The bones, muscles, tendons and ligaments of a horse adapt to the stresses placed upon them, making them stronger and more resilient. This process, known as Wolff's law for bones and the Davis's law for soft tissues, indicates that tissues adapt structurally to the forces they regularly encounter. However, excessive or improperly managed GRFs can lead to overuse injuries, underscoring the need for a balanced training regimen that promotes strength without causing harm.

IMPACT ON ENDURANCE

Endurance in horses relates to their ability to perform over extended periods. Efficient management of GRFs can enhance endurance by optimising energy use and minimising fatigue. When a horse moves, it must overcome the GRFs to propel itself forward. A horse that can do so efficiently will use less energy to complete the same amount of work as one that struggles with these forces. Furthermore, good biomechanics, including effective absorption and use of GRFs, can reduce wear and tear on the musculoskeletal system, delaying the onset of fatigue and reducing the risk of injury. This is particularly important in disciplines that require sustained effort, such as endurance racing or three-day eventing.

CONCLUSION

GRFs play a fundamental role in a horse's biomechanical health and performance. Understanding and optimising the interaction with these forces through proper training, conditioning and care can significantly impact a horse's balance, strength and endurance. It enables horses to move more efficiently, perform better and have longer, healthier careers. Paying close attention to how a horse interacts with the ground can also inform decisions about footwear, riding surfaces and training methods, all aimed at enhancing the horse's well-being and performance.

CHAPTER 10
THE NEUROSCIENCE OF HEALING

IT'S TIME TO TALK ABOUT PAIN What is pain? Pain is defined by the International Association for the Study of Pain (IASP) as, "an unpleasant sensory and emotional experience associated with actual or potential tissue damage or described in terms of such damage".

Pain is a useful mechanism as it warns us of harm. The brain has decided that you need protecting and has acted.

Clinical tip: Pain is normal. It is the most powerful protective mechanism that we have. Pain is like an early warning system when you touch something very hot or stand on something sharp. However, sometimes this signalling system becomes faulty and the stimulus for pain doesn't match the threat.

How does it work? Pain can originate from various sources within the body, including the skin, muscles, ligaments, joints, bones (nociceptive pain), injured tissues (inflammatory pain), nerves (neuropathic pain) or internal organs (visceral pain). Sometimes, pain may be a combination of these types, known as mixed pain. Even fascia (the connective bag of material fibres that keeps us together in a human shape) has pain receptors in it.

When pain occurs, nerve fibres transmit signals from the affected area through the spinal cord to the brain. However, in certain situations, such as after a stroke, damage to the brain or spinal cord itself can initiate the sensation of pain.

Upon reaching the brain, pain signals are processed and integrated with centres responsible for emotions, anxiety, sleep, appetite and memory.

The parts of the brain involved in pain responses are:

- Spinal cord: transmits pain signals from the body to the brain, and also plays a role in modulating these signals
- Hippocampus: involved in memory, fear conditioning and spatial awareness
- Cerebellum: controlling movement and cognition
- Hypothalamus and thalamus: autonomic regulation (adrenaline release), motivation and stress responses
- Primary somatosensory cortex: it discriminates sensory information from different parts of the body. It receives input from sensory receptors in the skin, muscles and joints.

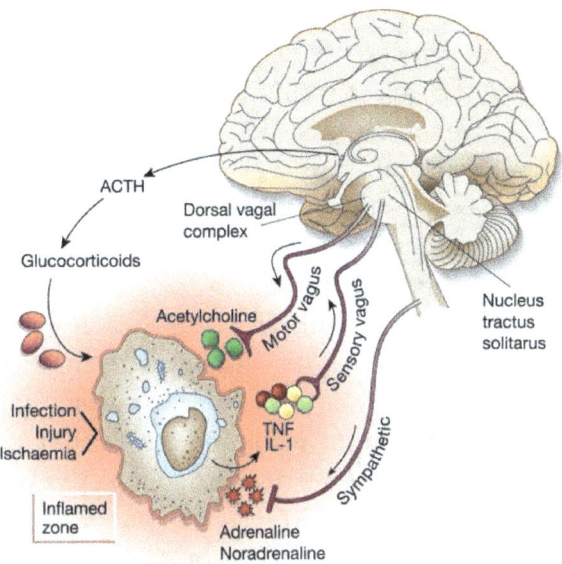

- Amygdala: is part of the Limbic system primarily involved in functions including memory, emotion and the body's fight-or-flight response. It allows us to remember painful stimuli and it can trigger a response upon exposure to those stimuli.
- Prefrontal cortex: involved with memory and problem solving
- Dorsal anterior Cingulate cortex and anterior cingulate cortex: connects actions into outcome learning, where we learn how to obtain our goals. They also affect our responses to physical pain. These areas also help us process social rejection.
- Premotor/motor cortex: where we prepare and organise for movement by selecting a plan of direction; the intention is created here based on external events, like visual cues.

This unique process results in a highly personalised experience of pain for each individual. Surprisingly, the amount of pain we perceive does not directly correlate to the amount of tissue damage or threat.

No two people's pains are alike, because no two people are the same. Our brains interpret the information sent via the spinal cord into the primary somatosensory cortex.

The emotional nature of pain makes it extremely difficult to create a one-size-fits-all model for recovery. There are many, many factors leading to the up regulation and down regulation of pain. The extent of emotional association and pain is often related to the context of the situation perceived. In other words, if you are anxious the pain can be worse, but the threat hasn't actually changed physically.

> **Clinical Tip:** Pain is never just "in the mind" or "just in the body". It is a complicated mixture of signals from the body and how the brain interprets them.
>
> Only you know your pain, even though it cannot be seen or measured. The challenge for both you and those treating you is to understand the complicated nature of persistent pain and the best way to manage it.

The role of your spinal cord in pain signalling

The spinal cord is a crucial component of the pain signalling pathway, playing a central role in transmitting pain signals from the body to the brain, and also in modulating those signals.

Here's a step-by-step explanation of how the spinal cord is involved in pain signalling:

1. **Detection of Painful Stimulus:** Pain begins with the detection of a noxious (harmful) stimulus by pain receptors (nociceptors) located in the skin, tissues, and organs. These receptors are sensitive to physical (e.g. cutting, burning), chemical (e.g. inflammatory mediators), and thermal (e.g. extreme heat or cold) stimuli that can cause tissue damage.
2. **Transmission to the Spinal Cord:** Once activated, nociceptors transmit pain signals through peripheral nerves towards the spinal cord. These signals enter the spinal cord through the dorsal horn, which is the rear part of the spinal cord and acts as a primary processing centre.
3. **Pain Signal Processing in the Dorsal Horn:** Within the dorsal horn of the spinal cord, the pain signal is modulated. This modulation involves several processes, including the release of neurotransmitters (like substance P and glutamate) and the activation of second-order neurons that carry the pain signal to the brain. The dorsal horn also contains circuits for the descending modulation of pain, which can inhibit or enhance pain signals based on input from the brain.
4. **Ascending Pathways to the Brain:** From the dorsal horn, pain signals are relayed to the brain through ascending pathways, primarily via the spinothalamic tract. This pathway projects to various brain regions, including the thalamus (which acts as a relay and

processing centre for sensory information), and from there to the cortex for pain perception, and to the limbic system, which is involved in the emotional aspects of pain.

5. **Descending Modulation of Pain:** The brain doesn't just passively receive pain signals; it actively modulates them through descending pathways. These pathways originate in the brainstem and project to the spinal cord, where they can enhance or inhibit pain signalling. This modulation is mediated by neurotransmitters and neuromodulators like endorphins (the body's natural painkillers), serotonin, and norepinephrine. This system can suppress the transmission of pain signals within the dorsal horn of the spinal cord, thereby reducing pain perception.

6. **Reflex Responses:** In addition to transmitting pain signals to the brain, the spinal cord also coordinates immediate reflex responses to pain, such as the withdrawal reflex. This is a protective mechanism where, for example, the spinal cord sends signals to muscles to contract and pull away from a painful stimulus (like touching a hot surface) even before the sensation of pain reaches the brain. In summary, the spinal cord is integral to pain signalling, serving both as a pathway for pain signals to reach the brain and as a centre for modulating these signals.

This dual role allows for the immediate protection from harmful stimuli and the nuanced perception and response to pain, including the potential for chronic pain conditions when these processes become dysregulated.

THE NEUROSCIENCE OF HEALING | 65

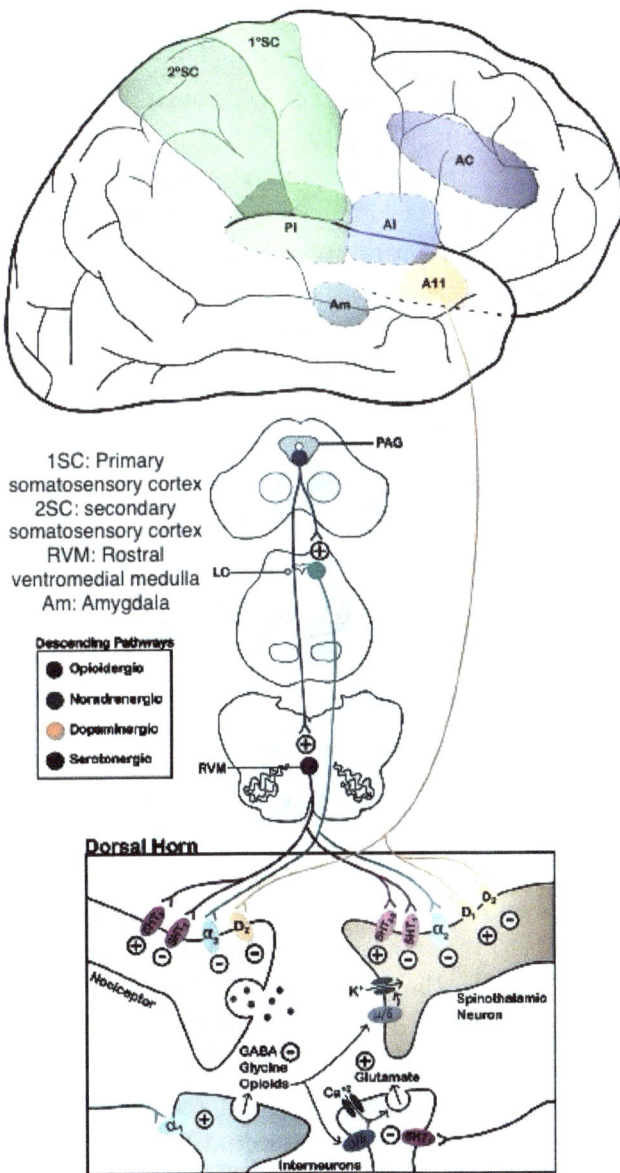

Image resource: Practical Neurology 2021, Vol 20, Deborah F. et al.

This image highlights the Pain signalling pathways from the sensory neurons and receptors through the spinal cord and into the brain.

This diagram shows the important areas in the effective processing of pain, including the pathways which modulate pain. These are the pathways that modern painkillers are often targeted on.

WHY IS BACK PAIN SO COMMON IN RIDERS?

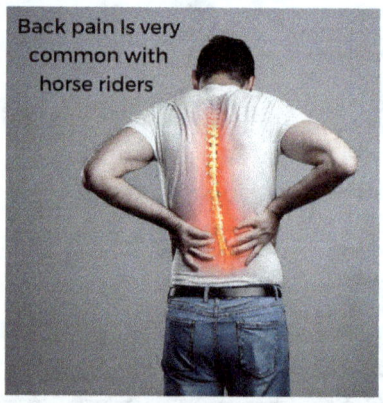

To understand this better, a short "anatomy lesson" is appropriate. The spine can be divided into two halves: front and back. The structures in the front half include the larger, heavier bones called vertebral bodies and the shock absorbing cushions that lie between the vertebral bodies called the intervertebral discs. The disc is like a jam doughnut where the centre is liquid-like and the outer portion is a tough, criss-cross pattern of cartilage arranged like the rings on a tree stump.

There are also ligaments that hold the vertebrae and discs tightly together. The back half of the spine includes the spinal cord and nerve roots, as well as the small joints of the back called facet joints. Every movable joint has a joint capsule (that helps lubricate the joint and limits the amount of movement) and surrounding ligaments.

The larger, heavier vertebral bodies and shock absorbing discs carry the majority of the weight (approximately 80%) while the smaller facet joints carry much less weight (only 20%) but are more responsible for guiding the movements of our back.

When leg pain is present, it can be caused by either a pinched nerve or an inflamed facet joint.

Clinical Tip: Not all leg pain means that you have sciatica! Often, it is due to referred pain on the lumbosacral joints, piriformis muscle or hip.

When a nerve is actually pinched (sciatica), the cause is usually from the intervertebral disc where the jelly-like centre leaks out and presses on the nerve that goes down the leg, commonly referred to as a herniated disc with sciatica. This type of pain is quite specific, easy to describe and often extends below the knee to the ankle or foot. It can include muscle weakness, numbness in certain areas of the leg and bending forward increases low back and leg

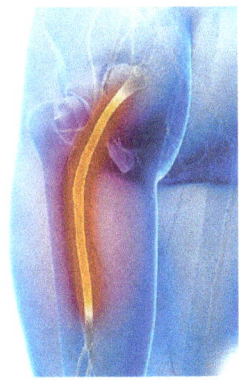

pain while bending backwards reduces the leg pain (and sometimes the low back pain).

When a facet joint capsule is affected, the pain is "referred" down the leg in a generalised, non-specific manner, usually described as a "deep ache", often hard to describe and usually the pain does not go below the level of the knee.

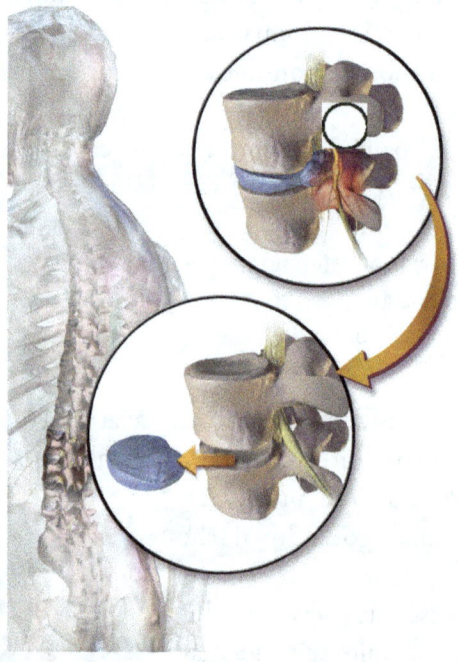

Image: the blue piece is the disc. The yellow wires are the nerves. The two blocks are the vertebral bodies.

The red circle is where the facet joint is located.

In the past surgeons used to remove damaged discs completely and fuse both vertebral bodies together. Fortunately, this is done very rarely now as it was often unsuccessful and caused a huge amount of restriction in the natural mechanics.

The good news is that both of these sources of low back and leg pain are very treatable with chiropractic care! The important point to remember is that getting prompt treatment when symptoms first appear is best because waiting and hoping it will subside on its own often results in the need for a longer course of treatment and is less satisfying for all concerned.

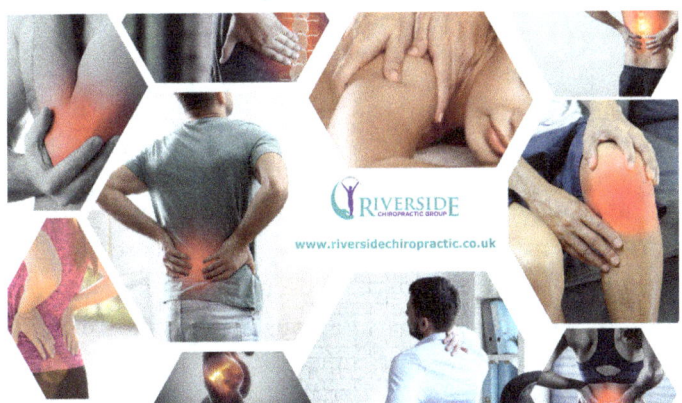

CHAPTER 11

THE NATURAL INFLAMMATORY CASCADE - SHOULD WE REALLY BE TRYING TO AVOID INFLAMMATION?

People suffering from new inflammation issues, such as after a fall, or who suffer from more chronic inflammatory disorders often take painkillers to alleviate the pain. While these drugs can decrease the suffering from pain, they do not eliminate the cause of the inflammation.

Treatments that target inflammation involve the use of synthetic steroids and a family of non-steroidal anti-inflammatory drugs (NSAIDS) both of which have many undesirable side effects. NSAIDS are widely used, especially for a variety of muscle and joint problems. These drugs inhibit the enzymes that are necessary for the formation of prostaglandins. While they may help in relieving symptoms, they also have negative health effects. The most serious and life-threatening side effect of

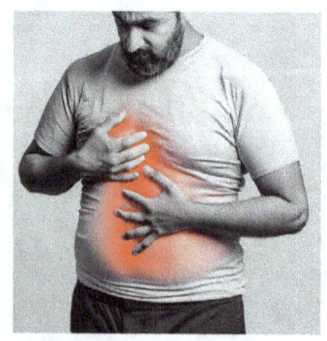

NSAIDS are gastrointestinal complications, such as bleeding.

THE LATEST NATURAL METHODS TO REDUCE PAIN AFTER AN ACCIDENT AND SPEED UP TISSUE HEALING CRYOTHERAPY

Inflammation management means <u>not</u> stopping the natural inflammatory process initiated by the body but controlling its over-activity. Ice immediately after a fall is good for pain relief but researchers warn of its negative effects on the body's natural healing response. Unfortunately, no one seems to agree on cold packs vs. heat packs. Both are good for reducing pain straight after an accident in non-open wounds. Most of the current research agrees that 15 minutes is the minimum time to achieve a therapeutic effect from an ice pack. Although I have found that people using them excessively has a negative effect and can cause an ice burn and nerve damage. I would recommend using them three time daily for 15 minutes, if using for pain relief purposes.

Researchers are still defining the optimum process and timing for cold-water immersion sessions. Although many sports medics and doctors still recommend using an ice bath at 5°C for three minutes, where the whole body is immersed, as it is said to have a much more stable result.

The research is currently undecided on an exact profile or gold standard for cold water immersion (CWI), but studies suggest utilising either full-body (excluding head) or limb-only immersion in water temperatures ranging between 40°F (5°C) and 68°F (20°C) for up to 20 minutes. This may be performed either continuously or intermittently. The main aim of CWI is to reduce body tissue temperatures and blood flow, which then leads to reductions in swelling, inflammation, cardiovascular strain and pain.

It is these physiological changes that lead to enhanced recovery by reducing hyperthermia-mediated fatigue, reducing the previously mentioned swelling and inflammation associated with delayed-onset muscle soreness (DOMS) and improving autonomic nervous system function.

At present there is no gold standard or optimal combination of water temperature, depth, duration and mode of immersion for CWI. The choice of protocol for CWI should vary depending on the athlete and what the athlete is recovering from.

COLD WATER SWIMMING – WHAT ARE THE BENEFITS?

Water should be 50°F (10°C) or colder. Keep in mind that the water in a frozen loch will be much colder. That's why it's a good idea to measure the temperature before you jump in. The plunge can be done as one continuous session or multiple sessions with breaks between the sessions.

Typically, cold-water plungers start with 30 seconds to a minute and work up to five to 10 minutes at a time. The most important aspect of CWI is getting your breathing techniques right. There are many clubs you can join in your local area where they can teach you safe immersion methods. The basics are to always enter the water on an exhale, which will provide room in the lungs to react to the

THE NATURAL INFLAMMATORY CASCADE - SHOULD WE REALLY BE TRYING TO AVOID INFLAMMATION? | 73

initial shock of immersion in cold water. When plunging into frigid temperatures, the nervous system causes the lungs to automatically take a big breath in, so having empty lungs will provide plenty of space for an inrush of oxygen. Then get into the water slowly. The shock of the cold will truly make you start to breathe rapidly at first, until you can slow down the rate. So, focus your mind on continuously taking slow deep breaths. Try to keep your attention on slowing your breathing down, and then over time try to last a little longer when it feels safe to do so each time. Continue increasing the time up to a maximum of five minutes.

The Wim Hof method asks you to take 30 quick breaths, then exhale and keep your lungs empty as long as possible. When you are gasping for air, take in a quick breath and hold it for 10 to 15 seconds. Then repeat this cycle three or four times. This technique will require a lot of practice and perseverance and should not be started without a cardiovascular exam by your GP.

RESTORATION OF INJURED TISSUES

Photo biomodulation (laser therapy), acupuncture, joint manipulation/mobilisation and specific soft tissue work.

The NICE guidelines in the UK are formed by the amalgamation of all the current research papers, usually using the best quality evidence like RCTs. In their guidelines they recommend joint manipulation, acupuncture and exercise for acute and chronic low back pain and headaches. https://www.nice.org.uk/guidance/ng59/resources/low-back-pain-and-sciatica-management-pdf-3531298536133

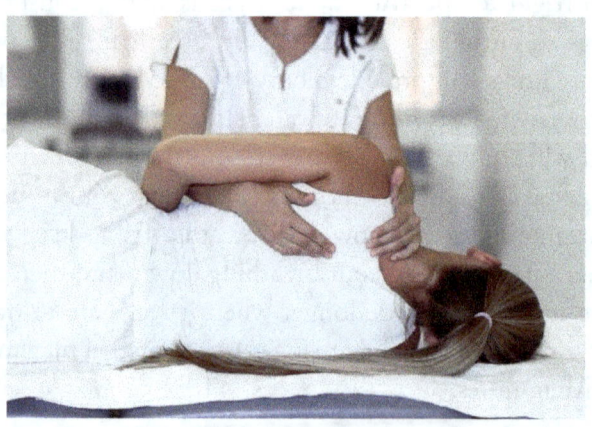

The most highly researched laser on the market is the Thor class 3b laser. It is used for tissue healing, pain relief, lymphatic drainage and more.

Tissue healing laser would be applied immediately and then daily for five days.

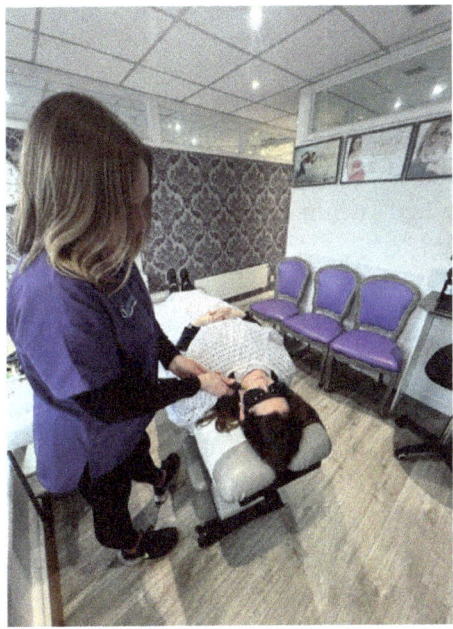

Joint manipulation and mobilisation after a fall are extremely beneficial when the joint is restricted, as the surrounding inflammation and muscle spasms will cause a lot of pain. Once the joint is able to move, it will start to heal the tissues more effectively. Ideally twice a week for two weeks including soft tissue work, Kinesio taping and laser combinations.

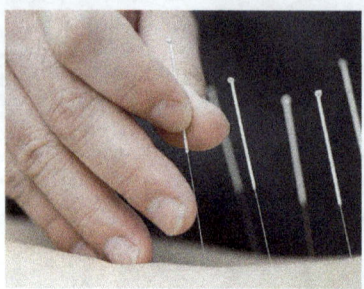 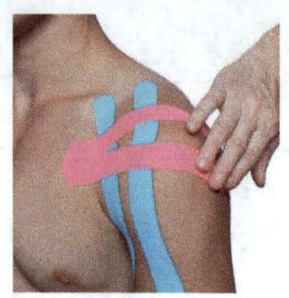

Acupuncture is an ideal modality to divert your brain's attention towards sites that require support to heal. It can also be utilised to reduce pain more naturally, especially for people with asthma or who are pregnant and cannot utilise NSAIDs.

SLEEP AND NATURAL RECOVERY

This allows the body to go through a natural healing cycle. This supports adaption and proper recovery of brain tissues, as well as the immune system (called innate immunity).

Ideally, most humans require eight hours of uninterrupted sleep. Although the circadian rhythm is what keeps us in a steady sleep cycle. Unfortunately, it can be altered by hormonal imbalances and synthetic medications.

> Clinical Tip: Sleep is your body's number one life hack to recovery". ☺
>
> Ideally, we require eight hours per night to get the most amount of natural, healthy sleep available for healing. Broken sleep is much more likely when you have pain. If the body is telling you to move, don't ignore it. Get up and move and use some cryotherapy to reduce your pain before trying to rest again.

SLEEP AND TISSUE HEALING

Focusing on tissue recovery, sleep plays a crucial role in healing and regeneration processes.

Here are five important factors highlighting the significance of sleep in tissue recovery:

1. **Human Growth Hormone (HGH) Release:** During deep sleep, the body releases human growth hormone, essential for tissue growth and repair. This hormone helps mend muscles and other tissues, supports bone health, and aids in the recovery process after injury.
2. **Inflammation Reduction:** Sleep can influence the levels of cytokines in the body, which are involved in inflammation. Proper sleep helps regulate these proteins, reducing inflammation and allowing for better recovery of tissues.
3. **Cell Regeneration:** Sleep enhances cellular regeneration processes. The body's cells, including those in muscles and other tissues, repair and regenerate more efficiently during sleep. This process is crucial for healing damaged tissues.
4. **Immune System Function:** Adequate sleep strengthens the immune system, which plays a direct role in tissue repair and fighting off infections that could complicate recovery. A well-functioning immune system ensures timely healing and regeneration of tissues.
5. **Stress Reduction**: Sleep helps regulate the body's stress response. Chronic stress can lead to elevated cortisol levels, which may impede tissue repair and recovery. By promoting relaxation and reducing stress, sleep facilitates a conducive environment for tissue healing.

Each of these factors underscores the interconnectedness of sleep with the body's healing processes, highlighting how essential quality sleep is for effective tissue recovery and overall health.

Chapter 12

Rebuilding Confidence After a Fall

A fall from a horse can be a significant setback, not just physically, but emotionally as well. For many riders, the journey back to full confidence is a challenging road paved with anxiety and fear. This chapter will explore the emotional hurdles that riders face after a fall and offer guidance on how to overcome them. We also discuss the usefulness of asking for help from a clinical psychologist.

Understanding the Impact of a Fall

The first step in overcoming the emotional impact of a horse-riding fall is understanding and acknowledging the feelings it can provoke. It's common to experience a range of emotions such as fear, anxiety, and even depression. These feelings are normal responses to a traumatic event and recognising them is crucial in the healing process.

The Role of a Clinical sports Psychologist

Our healthcare team includes a clinical psychologist who specialises in helping individuals recover from sports-related injuries. The psychologist works to address the mental and emotional aspects of recovery, which are often as critical as the physical healing. Here's how they can help:

Cognitive Behavioural Therapy (CBT)

CBT is a highly effective treatment for anxiety and is often used to help riders after a fall. This therapy focuses on changing negative thought patterns that can contribute to fear and anxiety. By challenging these thoughts, riders can gradually begin to replace fear with a more rational and confident mindset. In no way do any of these therapies imply that your thoughts and experiences are "all in your head", but the key to unlocking challenging thoughts definitely are processed and interpreted here. Which means that the answers and strategies for changing challenging thoughts often requires a little extra help from an expert with experience in helping you understand and unlock the answers.

Exposure Therapy: positive experiences

One method to help riders regain confidence is through controlled exposure to the source of their fear—the horse and the act of riding. This might start with simply visiting the stable and progressing to grooming the horse, followed by short, guided rides. The clinical psychologist and riding instructors will work together to create a safe, supportive environment for this exposure.

Relaxation Techniques

Techniques such as deep breathing, progressive muscle relaxation, and mindfulness can be taught by the psychologist to help manage anxiety symptoms. These tools are not only useful during the recovery process but are also valuable in everyday life, helping riders maintain a calm, focused state. An easy example of this would be the "square breathing" technique. You imagine breathing as the shape of a square where you breathe in and out for the same "length" of time. Ideally 3-5 secs for each side of the square until the shape has been completed in your mind. Yoga is an excellent way to focus our breathing and bring our attention back to our bodies to control our thoughts and emotions.

Build a Support System

Recovery is not a journey to be taken alone. It's essential to build a support system that includes family, friends, instructors, and healthcare professionals. Sharing your experiences and fears with others who understand can be incredibly comforting and empowering.

Set Realistic Goals

Setting achievable, incremental goals is crucial. Each small step forward can be a significant confidence builder. It might begin with simply watching others ride, then moving on to more direct interactions with the horse, and eventually returning to full riding. These goals should be set with the guidance of both the clinical psychologist and riding instructors to ensure they are both challenging and achievable.

If you fell off when hacking, take a supportive friend with a consistent horse who will help both you and your horse leave any post-traumatic feelings behind. Remind yourself what you loved about hacking before and take small steps to reaching that feeling once again. Freak accidents happen, it's not your fault. Don't let fear hold you back from what makes you happy. Although don't feel pressured to return to any sport before you feel physically ready. Your horse feels so much of your emotions and recognises your body language. Your partnership will help you both to heal together.

Celebrate the wins!

Progress is key to your recovery. Each milestone, no matter how small, is a victory and should be celebrated. This positive reinforcement helps build momentum and encourages continued progress.

Conclusion

Recovering from a horse-riding fall involves navigating both physical and emotional challenges. With the specialised help of a clinical psychologist, riders can address their fears and anxieties in a structured, supportive way. By understanding the emotional impacts, utilising therapeutic techniques, and leaning on a strong support network, riders can regain their confidence and return to riding with renewed strength and enjoyment.

Chapter 13

The fundamentals of Rider Safety a parents' guide

Discover essential tips and strategies in our comprehensive guide to help parents support their children's equestrian journey. Learn about safety practices, finding the right instructor, managing costs, and more.

COMMON TERMS USED IN EQUESTRIANISM AND THEIR MEANINGS

Navigating the world of equestrianism begins with understanding the language used within it. Here are some common terms and their meanings:

- ✓ Lead: The sequence of footfalls a horse uses at the canter and gallop. The leading leg is the one that strikes off first in front.
- ✓ Gait: Different ways a horse can move, including walk, trot, canter, and gallop.
- ✓ Tack: The equipment used on a horse, such as saddles, bridles, and reins.
- ✓ Bit: A metal mouthpiece on a bridle used to control a horse.

- ✓ Lunging: A training method where the horse moves in circles around the trainer on a long line.
- ✓ Farrier: A specialist in equine hoof care, including trimming and shoeing.
- ✓ Fore: Refers to the front part of the horse.
- ✓ Hind: Refers to the back part of the horse.
- ✓ Near: The left side of the horse when facing forward.
- ✓ Off: The right side of the horse when facing forward.
- ✓ Cantle: The back part of a saddle.
- ✓ Pommel: The front part of a saddle.
- ✓ Withers: The highest part of a horse's back, located between the shoulder blades.
- ✓ Hocks: The joint on a horse's hind leg located below the stifle.
- ✓ Fetlock: The joint located above the hoof.
- ✓ Pasterns: The area between the fetlock and the hoof.
- ✓ Ligaments: Connective tissue that connects bones to bones.
- ✓ Tendons: Connective tissue that connects muscles to bones.
- ✓ Joint: The location at which two or more bones make contact.
- ✓ Left Rein: The left side of the reins used to control the horse, also a description when moving the horse in a left circle.
- ✓ Right Rein: The right side of the reins used to control the horse, also a description when moving the horse in a right circle.
- ✓ Horse's Poll: The area right behind the horse's ears. It's actually the first neck vertebrae.

- ✓ Cross Pole Jump: A type of jump where two poles cross in the middle to form an "X".
- ✓ Straight Bar Jump: A jump consisting of a single horizontal bar.
- ✓ Oxer Jump: A jump made up of two parallel bars, making it wider.
- ✓ Dressage Test: A series of movements performed by the horse and rider, judged on precision and smoothness.
- ✓ Unaffiliated Class: A competition not recognised by the official governing body.
- ✓ Affiliated Class: A competition recognised by the official governing body.
- ✓ Horse Showing Class: A class in which horses are judged on appearance, manners, and performance.
- ✓ Horsemanship: The skill of handling, riding, and training horses.
- ✓ Equitation: The art and practice of horse riding, focusing on the rider's form and skill.

Understanding these terms is crucial for effective communication with instructors, coaches, and other equestrians, ensuring a safer and more productive learning experience for your child.

Useful Websites:
- [The Horse Glossary](https://www.thehorse.com/glossary)
- [Equine World UK](https://www.equine-world.co.uk)

TOP 5 THINGS TO LOOK FOR IN A GREAT RIDING COACH FOR YOUR CHILD

Choosing the right riding coach is crucial for your child's development and enjoyment in equestrianism. Here are the top five things to look for in a great riding coach:

1. Certification and Experience:
   - Accreditation: Ensure the coach has certification from a recognised equestrian organisation such as the British Horse Society (BHS), United States Pony Clubs (USPC), or the Professional Association of Therapeutic Horsemanship (PATH).
   - Experience: Look for a coach with extensive experience, especially in teaching children and beginners. An experienced coach will have a proven track record of helping young riders develop their skills safely and effectively.

2. Positive Teaching Style:
   - Patience and Encouragement: A great coach should be patient and encouraging, creating a supportive learning environment. They should be able to motivate your child and help them overcome challenges.
   - Clear Communication: The ability to communicate instructions clearly and effectively is essential. The coach should be able to explain techniques and concepts in a way that your child can understand and apply.

- Adaptability: The coach should adapt their teaching methods to suit your child's learning style and pace. Personalised instruction helps cater to individual needs and fosters better learning outcomes.

3. Safety-Focused Approach:
    - Emphasis on Safety: A great coach prioritises safety in all aspects of training. They should teach proper riding techniques, emergency dismounts, and the use of appropriate safety gear. They also should have an up-to-date first aid training certificate and a PVG safeguarding qualification.
    - Risk Management: The coach should be skilled in risk management, ensuring that the riding environment is safe and that horses used for lessons are well-trained and suitable for children.

4. Good Rapport with Children:
    - Building Trust: The coach should be able to build a trusting relationship with your child, making them feel comfortable and confident. This is essential for effective learning and enjoyment.
    - Positive Environment: Look for a coach who fosters a positive and inclusive atmosphere, where children feel valued and supported.

5. Clean and Well-Maintained Facilities:
    - Facility Standards: The riding facilities should be clean, well-maintained, and equipped with safe, reliable equipment. A well-kept facility reflects

the coach's professionalism and commitment to providing a quality learning environment.
- Horse Welfare: Ensure the horses used for lessons are healthy, well-cared for, and appropriate for your child's skill level. The coach should emphasise the importance of horse welfare in their teaching.

Additional Considerations:
- Progress Tracking: A great coach will track your child's progress and provide regular feedback. They should set achievable goals and celebrate milestones to keep your child motivated.
- Parental Involvement: The coach should welcome parental involvement and keep you informed about your child's development and any areas that need attention.
- References and Testimonials: Seek references and testimonials from other parents and students. Positive feedback from others can provide valuable insights into the coach's effectiveness and teaching style.

Useful Websites:
- [British Horse Society](https://www.bhs.org.uk)
- [United States Pony Clubs](https://www.ponyclub.org)
- [Professional Association of Therapeutic Horsemanship International](https://www.pathintl.org)
- [American Riding Instructors Association](https://www.riding-instructor.com)

- [The Pony Club UK](https://pcuk.org)
- [Association of British Riding Schools](https://www.abrs-info.org)
- [Equestrian Coaching Directory](https://www.equestriantrainingdirectory.co.uk)
- [British Equestrian Federation](https://www.britishequestrian.org.uk)

WHAT TO LOOK FOR IN SAFETY WEAR AND SAFETY STANDARDS IN 2024 FOR HAT AND BODY PROTECTORS VS AIR VESTS

Proper safety wear is crucial in preventing injuries while riding. Here's what you need to know about selecting the right equipment and understanding the latest safety standards.

1. Helmets:
   - Fit and comfort- helmets should fit snugly without being too tight. They should cover the forehead with the brim sitting about an inch above the eyebrows.
   - Safety standards - Look for helmets that meet the following Standards:
     1. PAS015:2011 (British standard)
     2. ASTM F1163 15 or later (US standard)
     3. VG1/EN1384:23 (EU standard, EN1384 replaced VG1 OCT 2023)
     4. Snell 2016/2021 (US standard)
     5. Quality Marks – Look for helmets that display the following Quality marks: BSI (British standards institute),

6. INSPEC (independent organization for the testing & certification of personal protective equipment &),
7. SEI (Safety equipment institute)
8. Snell

These quality marks ensures that:
1. Manufacturers have a portion of every batch they make tested.
2. In additional each model is also tested annually.
3. Manufacturers factories are rigorously audited annually.
4. Random Sample Testing (RST) can take place at any time.

Summary
1. Make sure it fits. If it isn't snug, it can move around and potentially reduce protection.
2. The more standards a helmet has, the more real-world accident scenarios it protects against. It is recommended that your helmet has 3 of the 4 standards listed for maximum protection.
3. Make sure it has a Quality mark. Most competitions will not allow you to compete without the relevant Quality mark, so it's very important to check what is required by the various equestrian associations.
4. Replacement: Helmets should be replaced after any significant impact, even if no damage is visible, as well as every five years due to wear and tear.

2. Body Protectors:
- Fit and Comfort: A body protector should fit snugly and cover the front and back of the torso, from the

collarbone to the lower rib cage. Adjustable straps can help achieve a secure fit.
- Safety Standards: Look for body protectors that meet the BETA Level 3 certification. This level offers the highest protection and is recommended for general riding, competitions, and working with horses.
- Types of Protectors: There are rigid and flexible body protectors. Choose one that offers a balance between protection and comfort, allowing for free movement.

3. Air Vests:
How They Work: Air vests are designed to inflate upon detecting a fall, providing additional protection for the spine, neck, and vital organs.
- Use with Body Protectors: Air vests should be used in conjunction with a traditional body protector for maximum safety.
- Standards and Certification: Ensure the air vest is CE certified, indicating it meets European safety standards.

4. Comparing Traditional Body Protectors vs. Air Vests:
- Traditional Body Protectors: Offer consistent protection and do not require activation. They are recommended for all types of riding.
- Air Vests: Provide additional protection but must be properly maintained and checked regularly. They are ideal for high-risk activities such as cross-country jumping but should not replace traditional body protectors.

5. Additional Safety Gear:
- Riding Boots: Proper riding boots should have a small heel to prevent the foot from slipping through the stirrup and provide ankle support.
- Gloves: Riding gloves enhance grip on the reins and protect the hands from blisters and injuries. They really hurt.
- Reflective Gear: If riding in low light conditions, use reflective vests or bands to increase visibility.

Discipline	British & European Standards	American Standards	Australian & New Zealand Standards
British Showjumping	PAS 015 (2011), VG1 (BSI Kitemarked)	SEI ASTM F1163 04a onwards, SNELL E2016	AS/NZS 3838 2006 onwards
British Dressage	PAS 015 (2011 and subsequent updates), VG1, EN1384:2023	SNELL E2016/E2021, ASTM F1163 2015 onwards	AS/NZS 3838 2006 onwards
British Eventing, Pony Club, British Riding Clubs, British Team Chasing	PAS 015 (2011), VG01.040 2014-12, BS EN1384:2023 (all with BSI Kitemark or Inspec IC Mark)	ASTM F1163 15 or 23 (SEI Mark), SNELL 2016/2021	AS/NZS 3838 2006 onwards (SAI Global Mark)

2024 Safety Standards:

1) Helmets: Must comply with updated ASTM/SEI or VG1 standards, which include enhanced impact testing.
2) Body Protectors: Only BETA level 3:2018 is now allowed in competition in the UK. This came into play in December 2023. It is also recommended to replace body and back protectors every 3-5 years. Most body protectors are designed to comply with EN13158 and a recognised BETA level standard. This standard encompasses three levels; we would always recommend riders to choose level three protectors as these offer the best protection and will meet the requirements for any equestrian discipline. https://beta-uk.org/wp-content/uploads/2024/10/

BETA-2018-Standard-updated-October-2022-with-label-costs-and-licensee-fee.pdf
3) Air Vests: Advancements in technology have led to quicker inflation times and better overall protection, with CE certification ensuring reliability.

By ensuring your child uses safety wear that meets these standards, you can significantly reduce the risk of injuries and provide a safer riding experience.

Useful Websites:
- [Helmet Safety Standards - SEI](https://www.seinet.org)
- [BETA Safety](https://www.beta-uk.org)
- [Riders4Helmets](https://www.riders4helmets.com)
- [British Equestrian Trade Association](https://www.beta-uk.org)

UNDERSTANDING COMMON TACK FOR HORSES

Understanding the various types of basic tack and their purposes is essential for ensuring your child's safety and the well-being of the horse. Here are the main components of horse tack, including different bits, nosebands, and saddle types:

Bits:
- Snaffle Bit: A simple, jointed bit that applies pressure on the horse's mouth to direct movement.
- Curb Bit: A leverage bit that exerts pressure on the horse's poll, chin, and mouth.

- Pelham Bit: A combination of snaffle and curb bit that provides more control.
- Gag Bit: A bit that applies pressure to the horse's mouth and poll, providing additional leverage for stronger control, often used for horses that pull or are strong.

Nosebands:
- Cavesson: A basic noseband that helps to keep the horse's mouth closed and the bit in place.
- Flash Noseband: Includes an additional strap to help prevent the horse from opening its mouth.
- Drop Noseband: Sits lower on the horse's nose to keep the mouth closed.
- Figure-Eight (Grackle) Noseband: Crosses over the nose to help control strong horses.

Saddle Types:
- English Saddle: Designed for various English riding disciplines, such as dressage and show jumping.
- Western Saddle: Built for comfort and security, commonly used in Western riding.
- Dressage Saddle: Designed for dressage, featuring a deep seat and long, straight flaps.
- Jumping Saddle: Lightweight with a forward-cut flap to accommodate shorter stirrups used in jumping.
- General Purpose (GP) Saddle: A versatile saddle designed for all-round use, suitable for both jumping and flatwork.
- VSD Saddle (Very Slightly Dressage): A multipurpose saddle with flaps that are slightly straighter than a

GP saddle, making it more suitable for flatwork and lower-level dressage while still being able to handle some jumping.

Assessing Correct Saddle Fit:

A correctly fitting saddle is crucial for both the rider's comfort and the horse's well-being. Here are key points to assess correct saddle fit:

1. Balance: The saddle should sit level on the horse's back.
2. Wither Clearance: There should be at least 2-3 fingers' width between the horse's withers and the saddle's pommel.
3. Panel Contact: The panels of the saddle should make even contact with the horse's back, without creating pressure points.
4. Gullet Width: The gullet should be wide enough to avoid pressure on the horse's spine.
5. Seat Size: The rider should have about a hand's width of space behind their seat when sitting in the saddle.
6. Movement: The saddle should remain stable when the horse moves, without shifting side to side or front to back.

Common Reasons for Saddles Slipping:

1. Poor Fit: An incorrectly fitted saddle is the most common reason for slipping.

2. Uneven Saddle Pad: A bunched-up or uneven saddle pad can cause slipping.
3. Loose/inappropriate Girth: Ensure the girth is tightened properly but not overly tight.
4. Horse Conformation: Some horses have conformation traits, like a high wither or a round barrel, that make saddle fitting more challenging.
5. Movement: The way a horse moves, especially if they have an exaggerated gait or are particularly round, can affect saddle stability.
7. Rider asymmetry. Not all riders sit with perfect posture. But the aim is to sit even and balanced. Using the seat and legs to steer and not the hands. The aids are essential to keep the horse in the correct shape to move forward in a good rhythm. Past lingering injuries, leg length issues, and muscle weaknesses or tension are some of the most common reasons for rider imbalances.

Each type of tack serves a specific purpose and should be chosen based on the horse's needs and the type of riding. Properly fitting tack is crucial to prevent discomfort and injury to the horse.

<u>Useful Websites</u>: Saddle Fitting Guide](https://www.thesaddleguide.com)

WHO ELSE CAN SUPPORT YOU?

In addition to veterinarians, several other healthcare professionals play crucial roles in maintaining a horse's health and well-being. Here's an overview of these professionals and their contributions:

1. Physiotherapist:
- Role: Helps with muscle issues and injuries through massage, stretching, and exercise programmes.
- Importance: Physiotherapists improve flexibility, strength, and recovery from injuries, enhancing overall performance and comfort.
- Useful Website: ACPAT (Association of Chartered Physiotherapists in Animal Therapy https://www.acpat.org

2. Chiropractor:
- Role: Aligns the horse's spine and joints through manual adjustments.
  - Importance: Chiropractors enhance mobility, alleviate pain, and improve overall spinal health, contributing to the horse's well-being and performance.
- Useful Website: [International Veterinary Chiropractic Association] https://ivca.de

3. Farrier:
- Role: Trims and shoes hooves to maintain hoof health and balance.
- Importance: Proper hoof care prevents lameness and supports the horse's overall health and soundness.

- Useful Website: [British Farriers and Blacksmiths Association](https://www.farrier-reg.gov.uk

4. Horse Dentist:
- Role: Ensures teeth are in good condition, performing dental check-ups and treatments.
- Importance: Regular dental care prevents eating problems, discomfort, and potential health issues related to poor dental health.
- Useful Website: [British Association of Equine Dental Technicians] https://www.baedt.com

5. Horse Nutritionist:
- Role: Develops diet plans tailored to the horse's specific needs, ensuring balanced nutrition.
- Importance: Proper nutrition is crucial for maintaining the horse's energy, health, and performance, preventing diet-related issues.

6. Bodywork and Rehab Practitioners:
- Role: Provide various therapeutic and medical services for horses, including musculoskeletal treatments.
- Importance: Practitioners address specific health issues, contribute to overall well-being, and support optimal performance.
- Useful Website: [RAMP (Register of Animal Musculoskeletal Practitioners) https://www.rampregister.org

KEEPING CHILDREN POSITIVE DURING EMOTIONALLY CHALLENGING DAYS

Riding and working with horses can be both exhilarating and frustrating, especially for young riders. Here are some strategies to help keep children positive and motivated, even on challenging days:

1. Open Communication:
- ✓ Encourage Expression: Allow your child to express their feelings about their riding experiences, whether they are positive or negative.
- ✓ Active Listening: Listen attentively to their concerns and frustrations without immediately offering solutions. Sometimes, they just need to feel heard.

2. Set Realistic Goals:
- ✓ Small Achievements: Break down larger goals into smaller, achievable milestones. Celebrate these small successes to build confidence.
- ✓ Personal Progress: Focus on individual progress rather than comparing your child to others. Every rider advances at their own pace.

3. Positive Reinforcement:
- ✓ Praise Effort: Acknowledge and praise the effort your child puts into their riding, regardless of the outcome.
- ✓ Rewards System: Implement a rewards system for achieving certain milestones or demonstrating perseverance and good sportsmanship.

4. Balance and Variety:
- ✓ Mix Activities: Include a variety of activities within their riding schedule, such as trail rides, fun games, or groundwork with the horse.
- ✓ Breaks and Rest: Ensure your child takes regular breaks to rest and avoid burnout. It's essential to maintain a balance between riding and other activities.

5. Supportive Environment:
- ✓ Positive Atmosphere: Surround your child with supportive peers and mentors who encourage and uplift them.
- ✓ Constructive Feedback: Ensure that feedback from instructors is constructive and focused on improvement rather than criticism.

6. Fun and Enjoyment
- ✓ Keep It Fun: Remember to keep the riding experience enjoyable. Introduce fun challenges or themed riding days to keep your child engaged.
- ✓ Horse Bonding: Encourage your child to spend time bonding with their horse outside of riding, such as grooming or hand-walking, to build a stronger connection.

7. Managing Frustration:
- ✓ Teach Resilience: Help your child understand that setbacks are a natural part of learning and growth. Teach them resilience and coping strategies for handling frustration.

✓ Positive Mindset: Encourage a positive mindset by focusing on what can be learned from difficult experiences rather than dwelling on mistakes.

8. Role Models and Inspiration:
✓ Inspirational Stories: Share stories of accomplished riders who faced challenges and persevered. Role models can provide motivation and a sense of possibility.
✓ Visual Motivation: Use vision boards or journals where your child can track their goals, achievements, and dreams related to riding.

By employing these strategies, you can help your child stay positive and motivated, even during emotionally challenging days. This not only enhances their enjoyment of riding but also builds their resilience and confidence in handling setbacks.

Useful Websites:
- [Psychology Today](https://www.psychologytoday.com)
- [Positive Parenting Solutions](https://www.positiveparentingsolutions.com)
- [Your Horse Magazine - Tips for Motivation](https://www.yourhorse.co.uk)

CONCLUSION

Equestrianism offers numerous benefits, from physical exercise and mental stimulation to the joy of bonding with a horse. However, it also requires a significant commitment of time, effort, and resources. By understanding the essential aspects covered in this chapter, parents can ensure their children have a safe and fulfilling equestrian experience. From learning common terms and selecting the right tack to finding a great instructor and maintaining safety, each element plays a crucial role in fostering a positive environment for young riders.

Additionally, knowing when it's time to get your own pony and how to manage the associated costs ensures that the experience is both enjoyable and sustainable. By leveraging local marketplace platforms, sharing resources, and utilising the services of various healthcare professionals, parents can effectively support their children's equestrian journeys.

Remember, the ultimate goal is to keep children safe, motivated, and happy while they pursue their passion for riding. By following the guidelines and tips provided in this chapter, parents can help their children navigate the exciting world of equestrianism with confidence and care.

Summary of Key Points:

1. Common Terms Used in Equestrianism: Understanding key terms helps in effective communication and ensures better learning.
2. Common Tack for Horses: Properly fitted tack is crucial for the comfort and safety of both horse and rider.
3. Finding the Right Instructor: A certified, experienced, and supportive instructor can significantly impact a child's riding experience.

4. Avoiding Serious Injuries: Emphasising safety practices and proper training helps prevent accidents and injuries.
5. Safety Wear Standards: Investing in certified safety gear, including helmets and body protectors, is essential for protecting young riders.
6. Keeping Children Positive: Open communication, realistic goals, positive reinforcement, and a supportive environment are key to maintaining motivation and enjoyment.
7. Getting Your Own Pony: Assessing commitment, skill level, financial capability, and readiness helps in making informed decisions about pony ownership.
8. Saving Money: Using local marketplace platforms, sharing resources, and managing unexpected costs effectively helps in reducing overall expenses.
9. Healthcare Professionals for Horses: Regular care from physiotherapists, Chiropractors, farriers, dentists, and nutritionists is essential for maintaining a horse's health and performance.

By following these comprehensive guidelines, parents can create a safe, supportive, and enriching environment for their children's equestrian pursuits, ensuring that they enjoy all the benefits of this rewarding activity.

Useful Websites list
- [The Horse Glossary](https://www.thehorse.com/glossary)
- [Equine World UK](https://www.equine-world.co.uk)

- [SmartPak Equine Tack Guide](https://www.smartpakequine.com)
- [Dover Saddlery](https://www.doversaddlery.com)
- [United States Pony Clubs](https://www.ponyclub.org)
- [British Horse Society](https://www.bhs.org.uk)
- [Association of British Riding Schools](https://www.abrs-info.org)
- [The Pony Club UK](https://pcuk.org)
- [Equestrian Coaching Directory](https://www.equestriantrainingdirectory.co.uk)
- [British Equestrian Federation](https://www.britishequestrian.org.uk)
- [Riders4Helmets](https://www.riders4helmets.com)
- [Equestrian Safety](https://www.equestriansafety.com)
- [Psychology Today](https://www.psychologytoday.com)
- [Positive Parenting Solutions](https://www.positiveparentingsolutions.com)
- [Your Horse Magazine - Tips for Motivation](https://www.yourhorse.co.uk)
- [Equine.com](https://www.equine.com)
- [Horse and Rider](https://www.horseandrider.com)
- [American Association of Equine Practitioners](https://www.aaep.org)
- [The Horse Vet Corner](https://www.thehorse.com)
- [British Equine Veterinary Association](https://www.beva.org.uk)
- [British Farriers and Blacksmiths Association](https://www.farrier-reg.gov.uk)
- [British Equine Dental Association](https://www.baedt.com)

- [ACPAT (Association of Chartered Physiotherapists

  in Animal Therapy)](https://www.acpat.org)
- [International Veterinary Chiropractic Association] (https://ivca.de)
- [Royal Agricultural University Nutritionists Register] (https://www.rampregister.org)
- [RAMP (Register of Animal Musculoskeletal Practitioners)](https://www.rampregister.org)

AN AMATEUR'S GUIDE TO EQUESTRIAN SUCCESS

Success in equestrian sports is like a custom-fit saddle – it looks different for everyone. For some, it's the confidence that comes from knowing you've given it your all. For others, it's the contentment of mastering a new skill or the thrill of clinching a trophy or medal.

Many equestrians, especially amateurs, tend to put undue pressure on themselves to emulate top riders. It's worth remembering that even the best started as novices, dealing with the same spills and thrills you're experiencing now. They've just had more time to learn from their mistakes, work with coaches, and refine their skills.

THE NOVICE ADVANTAGE

Young riders might not have as many scars of doubt, but they also lack the core stability, strength, and breadth of knowledge that comes with experience. As an amateur rider myself, I've invested countless hours and dollars in lessons, seeking guidance from more experienced riders and instructors. Riding, much like biochemistry (shoutout to my undergrad prof!), is a perpetual learning process.

We're always evolving our techniques for the horse's benefit, gaining insight into their psychology and biomechanics to forge a better partnership. These magnificent creatures have graciously allowed us into their world; it's our duty to nurture and harmonise with them.

DEFINING SUCCESS IN EQUESTRIAN SPORTS

Success isn't just about winning. It's about personal growth, consistency, effort, and resilience. Riders often get caught in the pursuit of rosettes without challenging themselves to improve, leading to self-doubt and insecurity. Finding the right instructor is crucial, whether you're competing at FEI level or local shows.

THE DONKEY, THE CARROT, AND THE STICK

Have you heard the one about the donkey? Picture this:
- The Donkey represents an individual striving for a goal.
- The Carrot symbolises positive reinforcement, the rewards that pull us forward.
- The Stick stands for negative reinforcement, the push to avoid negative outcomes.

Using both the carrot and the stick can be a balanced approach to motivation. Personalising this balance is key; some respond better to rewards, others to the fear of consequences.

Real-Life Examples
In sports, an athlete might be driven by the carrot of winning a championship and the stick of disappointing their team. In business, an employee might strive for a promotion (carrot) while avoiding poor performance reviews (stick).

OVERCOMING FEAR AVOIDANCE TACTICS

Fear avoidance can hinder progress. Common tactics include:
- Avoiding Competition: Skipping events to dodge pressure.
- Limiting Practice: Shying away from challenging drills.
- Over-Caution: Playing it too safe.

- Negative Self-Talk: Doubting oneself to justify avoidance.

STRATEGIES TO CONQUER FEAR

1. Goal Setting: Focus on specific, process-oriented goals.
2. Gradual Exposure: Face fears progressively.
3. Mental Skills Training: Use visualisation and positive self-talk.
4. Cognitive-Behavioural Techniques: Reframe thoughts and employ relaxation strategies.
5. Support Systems: Lean on coaches and peers.
6. Education: Learn about injury prevention and performance psychology.
7. Professional Help: Consult a sports psychologist if needed.

By addressing these tactics, riders can enhance their mental resilience and performance, leading to greater personal development.

Conclusion

Remember, success in equestrian sports is about more than just winning. It's about the journey, the learning, and the bond with your horse. Whether you're motivated by the carrot, the stick, or a bit of both, embrace the process, and don't let fear hold you back. Enjoy the ride!

CHAPTER 14
HEALTH – WHAT DOES THAT ACTUALLY MEAN?

Let me ask you this. Does health mean the absence of disease or does it mean that your system is functioning optimally?

Is someone who isn't in constant pain healthy? Is someone who isn't overweight healthy?

In actual fact, health is a dynamic process that requires regular cycles of wakeful activity and restorative sleep. Our best healing occurs during our sleeping hours.

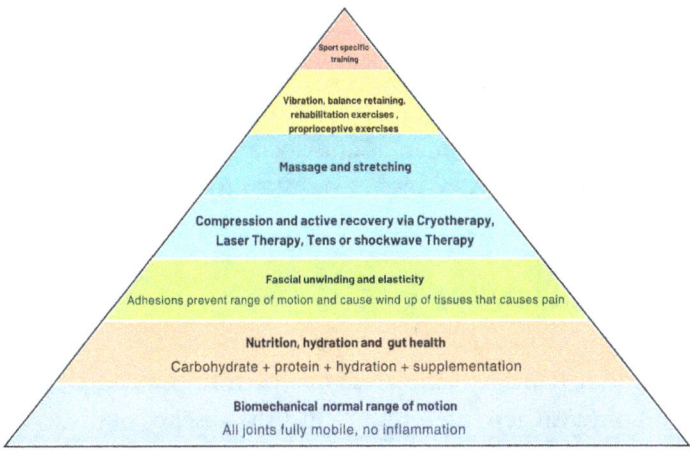

The recovery pyramid. The foundation for all future success is based on biomechanics first.

The ideal strategy for a healthy body would look like this pyramid above with functional neuromuscular homeostasis being the foundation for success.

"The inability of antibiotics to wipe out disease entirely and the emergence of antibiotic resistant bacteria and super infections have led many distinguished researchers and physicians to conclude that the answer to disease is not to create stronger medicines. Rather, we say the solution lies in attacking the disease from the inside out by strengthening the body's natural defense network."

Dr Robert Roundtree, Immunotics

Health is a multifaceted concept that transcends the mere absence of disease or the perception of pain. The World Health Organization (WHO) defines health as "a state of complete physical, mental and social well-being and not merely the absence of disease or infirmity". This definition highlights that health encompasses a broad spectrum of dimensions:

Physical Health: This involves the proper (optimum) functioning of the body's systems, being free from illness, injury or pain, and the ability to perform everyday tasks and physical activities. It's not just the absence of diseases, but also includes physical fitness and vitality.

Mental Health: Mental health refers to a person's psychological and emotional well-being. It's about how individuals think, feel and behave, how they cope with life's stresses, make decisions and interact with others. Good mental health isn't just the absence of mental disorders or disabilities.

Social Well-being: This dimension of health concerns individuals' ability to form satisfying interpersonal relationships with others and to adapt to various social situations and roles. It involves the community and environment's impact on health, as well as the impact of a person's behaviour on the community's well-being.

Spiritual Health: For some, spiritual health is also an important aspect of overall well-being, involving values and beliefs that help provide a purpose in life. It may involve religious faith, but it also encompasses personal peace, harmony and a sense of balance in life.

Health, therefore, is a dynamic and continuous state, involving the maintenance and improvement of one's physical, mental and social well-being. It requires attention to lifestyle and societal factors, as well as the healthcare needs that can prevent diseases and maintain optimal well-being. The perception of pain or the absence of disease might be indicators of health, but do not fully capture the essence of what it means to be healthy.

Health is more about the ability to lead a rich, fulfilling life in all its dimensions.

WHAT IS STRESS AND WHEN IS IT USEFUL?

When considering stress, it's common to associate it with an emotional reaction. However, stress encompasses various challenges that our bodies encounter routinely. These challenges include external stressors such as injuries, which prompt our bodies to mobilise defences like antibodies to address foreign invaders.

Additionally, internal stressors, such as compromised immune function, can trigger responses like the release of harmful substances like free radicals within our cells. Furthermore, physical and emotional stresses contribute to the overall burden on our immune system, highlighting the multifaceted nature of stress on our health.

But what happens if our cells inside our bodies are under stress? Stress can be actuated from physical stress, a pain response, an emotional response, chronic inflammation or immune-mediated.

CHAPTER 15
THE BIOCHEMISTRY OF HEALING

The newest research focuses on a pathway called CDR1-3.

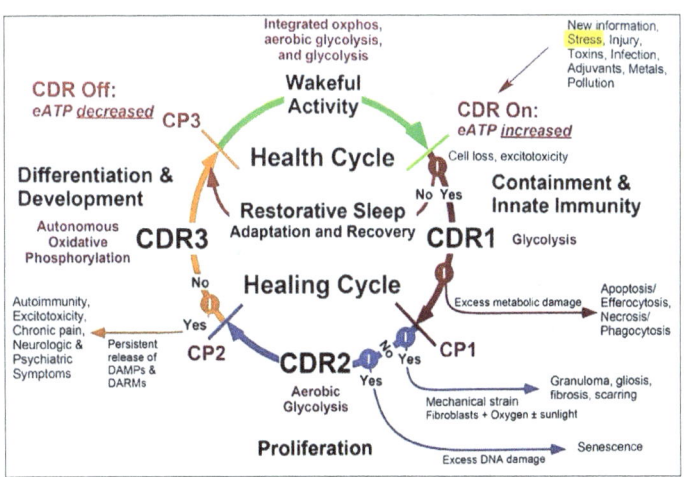

CDR1 means containment and innate immunity (glycolysis). Cellular glycolysis is a fundamental metabolic process occurring in the cytoplasm of cells, essential for energy production and the generation of building blocks for other biochemical pathways.

In glycolysis, a single molecule of glucose is broken down into two molecules of pyruvate through a series of enzymatic reactions. This process generates a small amount of ATP, the cell's primary energy currency, and NADH, a coenzyme involved in various cellular processes. Glycolysis serves as a central pathway for both aerobic and anaerobic metabolism, playing a crucial role in sustaining cellular energy levels and supporting diverse cellular functions.

CDR2 means cell proliferation and cellular regeneration. Cellular proliferation refers to the process by which cells multiply and divide, leading to an increase in cell numbers. This fundamental biological process is essential for growth, tissue repair and the maintenance of homeostasis within organisms.

Aerobic glycolysis, also known as the Warburg effect, is a metabolic phenomenon where cells preferentially use glycolysis for energy production even in the presence of oxygen. This process involves the conversion of glucose into pyruvate, followed by the conversion of pyruvate into lactate, generating a small amount of ATP. Aerobic glycolysis is commonly observed in rapidly proliferating cells, such as cancer cells, and is believed to support their increased energy demands and biosynthetic needs for growth and proliferation.

CDR3 means differentiation and development, involving Autonomous Oxidative Phosphorylation. This begins once cell proliferation has stopped. New cells can then take on their new role (specific organic functions). In other words, new cells are created and given a job to do by their boss cells. It's an amazingly intricate system.

WHAT REDUCES OUR BODY'S ABILITY TO HEAL?

Poor gut function has been shown to directly affect nervous system function which can affect tissue healing response. Emerging research has shown that IBS may be caused by problems in the nervous system pathways that connect the gut and the brain. This is why people describe situations that make them nervous or anxious as "gut-wrenching" and "butterflies in the stomach", etc. There is an emotional sensitivity to our gastrointestinal tract. Obviously, the brain has a direct effect on both the stomach and intestines. For example, at the very thought of eating, the gut will begin to release more fluids to break down the foods before they even enter our mouths.

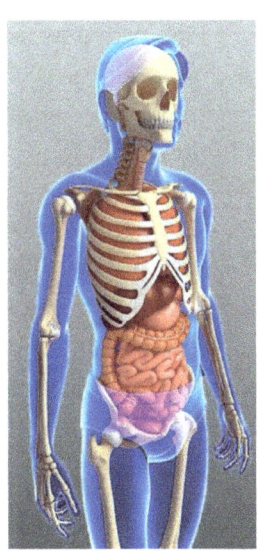

Why? Poor gut function and chronic gut inflammation can negatively impact tissue healing due to several interconnected factors:

Nutrient Absorption: A compromised gut function may impair the absorption of essential nutrients required for tissue repair and regeneration, such as vitamins, minerals and amino acids.

Immune Response: Gut inflammation can trigger systemic inflammation and dysregulate the immune system, diverting resources away from the healing process towards combating inflammation.

Microbiome Dysbiosis: Imbalances in the gut microbiome, often associated with gut inflammation, can disrupt the production of beneficial metabolites and signalling molecules crucial for tissue repair.

Increased Oxidative Stress: Gut inflammation can lead to the production of reactive oxygen species (ROS) and oxidative stress, which can hinder cellular functions involved in tissue healing and regeneration.

Delayed Wound Healing: Inflammatory signalling pathways activated in the gut can interfere with the normal progression of wound healing, leading to delays in the resolution of tissue damage.

> **Clinical Tip:** Addressing gut health and inflammation through dietary modifications, probiotics and anti-inflammatory interventions can support tissue healing and overall health.

Kitchen Clean-Out

Do you want to maximize your chances of success? Especially if you have difficult cravings/sugar addiction, it is smart to throw out (or give away) sugary and starchy foods, low-fat products, etc. Here's a list of what to get rid of:

Pantry
Candy
Chocolate
Cookies
Sugar in all forms
Muffins
Breakfast cereals
Potato chips
Popcorn
Snacks (dried fruits etc.)
Crackers
Wheat flour
Pasta
Rice
Potatoes
Beer
Bagels
Bread
Fruit
Soup cans
Beans

Fridge
Soft drinks and fruit juices
Applesauce
Jams
Margarine
Everything that says "low fat" or "no fat"
Ketchup
Bottled sauces
Ready made spice mixes (taco, bbq, fajita etc.)
Ready made salsas

Freezer
Ice cream
Buns
Cakes
Ready made waffles

Why not do it now?

PREBIOTICS AND PROBIOTICS: UNDERSTANDING THE BASICS

Prebiotics are a type of dietary fibre that the human body cannot digest. They serve as food for probiotics, which are live microorganisms that provide health benefits when consumed. Probiotics can be found in foods such as yogurt, sauerkraut and tempeh, and are also available as dietary supplements. They play a crucial role in maintaining a healthy gut microbiota by reducing pathogenic microbes, enhancing immune response and improving the intestinal barrier function.

THE ROLE OF GUT HEALTH IN ATHLETIC PERFORMANCE AND RECOVERY

Gut health is crucial for overall well-being, and it plays a significant role in athletic performance and injury recovery. A healthy gut microbiome can help reduce oxidative stress and inflammation, aiding in faster recovery from muscle damage. It's particularly important for athletes, including equestrians, who undergo intense and prolonged physical activity, as this can affect gut health and lead to gastrointestinal issues.

RECENT RESEARCH ON PROBIOTICS AND PREBIOTICS

There's substantial evidence supporting the effectiveness of probiotics in treating various gastrointestinal disorders and reducing the incidence of upper respiratory tract infections. Certain strains of probiotics, known as psychobiotics, have also shown potential in improving mental health conditions such as depression and anxiety. However, it's crucial to note that the health benefits of probiotics are strain and dose dependent.

https://www.4thdiscipline.com/blog/prebiotics-and-probiotics-for-athletes

INCORPORATING PREBIOTICS AND PROBIOTICS INTO AN EQUESTRIAN'S DIET

Athletes, including equestrians, can benefit from incorporating prebiotic- and probiotic-rich foods into their diets. Fermented foods such as yogurt, kefir, sauerkraut and kimchi are excellent sources of probiotics. Meanwhile, prebiotics can be found in foods like bananas, onions, garlic and wholegrains. For those considering supplements, it's recommended to choose products based on scientific research, ensuring they contain viable strains of bacteria and enough colony-forming units (CFUs).

For equestrians, understanding the role of prebiotics and probiotics in promoting gut health, enhancing performance and supporting recovery is essential. By focusing on a diet rich in these components or considering supplementation, athletes can leverage the health benefits of a balanced gut microbiome. Future research may unveil even more potential benefits and applications of prebiotics and probiotics in sports nutrition.

We often recommend Biocare products in our clinics, as they have excellent properties for probiotics and are specific for different age groups' requirements.

https://www.biocare.co.uk/categories/live-bacteria

A daily dose has enough bacteria to establish a healthy colony for improved gut function and immunity.

The intricate relationship between our gut and brain, often referred to as the gut-brain axis, has garnered significant attention in the field of neuroscience and holistic health. Emerging research continues to underscore the profound impact that gut health has on our mental wellbeing, highlighting the importance of nurturing this symbiotic relationship for optimal cognitive function and emotional balance.

THREE LIFE HACKS TO BOOST GUT HEALTH

1) **Mindful eating:** Cultivate a deeper awareness of the foods you consume and their effects on your body and mind. By prioritising whole, nutrient-dense foods and minimising processed and inflammatory ingredients, you can promote a healthy gut microbiome and support optimal brain function. Take time to savour each bite, chew slowly, and listen to your body's hunger and fullness cues.
2) **Buy naturally probiotic-rich foods:** Add yogurt, kefir, sauerkraut and kimchi into your diet. These fermented delicacies are teeming with beneficial bacteria that help maintain a balanced gut microbiome, which in turn can positively influence mood, cognition and overall mental health. Experiment with different varieties and flavours to find what resonates with your palate.

3) **Stress management techniques:** Prioritise stress-reducing activities such as meditation, deep breathing exercises, yoga or spending time in nature. Chronic stress can disrupt the delicate balance of the gut-brain axis, leading to inflammation, digestive disturbances and mood imbalances. By incorporating regular relaxation practices into our daily routines, we can support a harmonious connection between our gut and brain and cultivate resilience in the face of life's challenges.

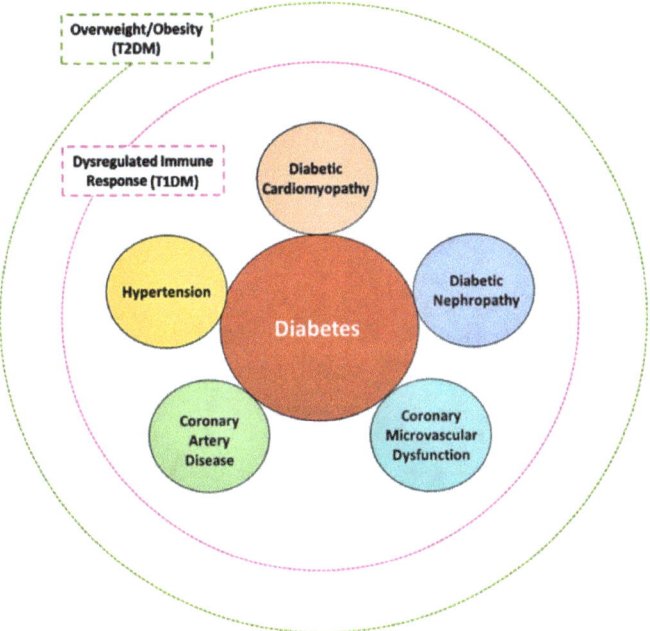

Source: Journal of clinical medicine 2021, 10(16), 3682.

By nurturing our gut health and fostering a holistic approach to wellness, we can optimise our mental clarity, emotional resilience and overall vitality. Let's harness the power of the gut-brain connection to unlock our full potential and thrive in every aspect of our lives.

Some chronic disease processes like diabetes affect wound healing due to a complex pathophysiological pathway involving vascular, neuropathic and immune components. This directly affects the speed at which someone can heal and can make diabetic people susceptible to complications. In other words, high levels of insulin in the bloodstream causes white blood cell function to become impaired. White blood cells are essential for immune system health.

CHAPTER 16
MUSCLE HEALTH

Loss of muscle mass and strength can make it harder to carry out daily activities leading to a lower quality of life. It can also increase the risk of falls and fractures, which can lead to a loss of independence.

Muscle health, nutrition and ageing are all linked

Muscle health is associated with ageing and physical inactivity. Not eating a nutrient-rich diet can also lead to a decline in muscle health. Food and drink are fuel for our bodies. Without the right type of fuel, our bodies struggle to work at their best. Good nutrition plays an important role in helping you to maintain healthy strong muscles and bones, and with that comes a reduced risk of falls.

> **Clinical Tip:** Resistance activities increase muscle strength by making your muscles work against a weight or force. Regular resistance activities and a nutrient-rich diet is the ideal combination.
>
> Based on the research, resistance training offers numerous benefits that are particularly relevant to horse riders seeking to improve their muscle health and prevent falls.

SUMMARY OF KEY FINDINGS

General Benefits of Resistance Training: Resistance training can significantly enhance muscle strength, stamina and overall physical performance. It's beneficial for improving mobility, balance, posture and decreasing the risk of injury. This form of exercise also plays a crucial role in preventing or controlling chronic conditions like diabetes, heart disease, arthritis, back pain, depression and obesity. Moreover, it aids in pain management, increases bone density and improves mental wellbeing, including self-esteem and mood. The practice of resistance training, through its varied exercises, repetitions and sets, ensures progressive muscle strengthening and recovery, vital for every fitness regime.

Clinical Tip: Given these benefits, horse riders can greatly enhance their muscle strength, balance and overall physical conditioning through tailored resistance training workouts. This not only helps in preventing falls, but also improves riding performance and health outcomes.

Resistance training has been shown to combat the loss of muscle mass that typically occurs with age, enhancing lean weight and boosting resting metabolic rate. It also contributes to improved cognitive abilities, movement control, walking speed and functional independence. This type of training is pivotal for the prevention and management of type 2 diabetes by improving insulin sensitivity and cardiovascular health. Additionally, resistance training promotes bone development and can alleviate symptoms of low back pain, arthritis and fibromyalgia, making it a comprehensive approach to reversing age-related declines in muscle health.

Based on recent studies, the effectiveness of resistance training protocols in building muscle strength and endurance has been closely examined, revealing insightful strategies for athletes, including horse riders. One study compared the effects of different repetition maximum (RM) resistance training protocols on muscle volume and strength over a 10-week period. The findings suggest that both high-load low-repetition (7 sets of 4 reps) and intermediate-load intermediate-repetition (4 sets of 8 reps) protocols significantly improve muscle strength, with notable increases in 1-RM strength. These increases were attributed to muscle hypertrophy as well as neuromuscular adaptations, indicating the importance of varying sets, reps and intensities in a training programme to achieve optimal strength and hypertrophy gains.

In addition to strength training, incorporating endurance training into an athlete's regimen, especially for those involved in sports that require sustained performance, has been studied. Concurrent training, which involves both endurance and strength training, does not necessarily negate strength gains when cycling is used as the endurance component. This approach allows athletes to target cardiovascular health and muscle endurance without significantly impacting strength development. However, the programming of endurance and strength training sessions should be carefully considered, with recommendations suggesting a focus on strength and hypertrophy training before endurance work to minimise interference effects. For those aiming to improve power, high-intensity interval training (HIIT) can be an effective method to develop both power and stamina when placed before strength training in a session.

These insights into the latest research on building muscle strength and endurance emphasise the benefits of a well-rounded training programme that includes both resistance and endurance training, tailored to the specific demands of the athlete's sport. For horse riders, focusing on resistance training that enhances strength and neuromuscular adaptations, while also incorporating elements of endurance training, can contribute to improved performance and injury prevention.

Creating a 7-day resistance training workout plan for horse riders involves focusing on overall strength, stability, balance and endurance, tailored to support the unique demands of horse riding. Here's a structured plan incorporating rest and varied intensity levels to optimise recovery and performance gains, leveraging insights from resistance and endurance training research.

Focusing on lower abdominal strength is key for core stability, improving posture, enhancing athletic performance and reducing the risk of back pain.

TEN OF THE BEST EXERCISES SPECIFICALLY AIMED AT STRENGTHENING THE LOWER ABDOMINALS

1. **Leg raises:** Lie flat, raise your legs straight up and then lower them without touching the floor. This targets the lower abs directly.
2. **Single leg bridges**: Lie on your back, lift your pelvis from neutral into a bridge, then raise one leg to 90 degrees by lifting that foot off the floor without twisting through your middle or dropping your hips on one side. If you get cramp in the back of your thigh then your glute isn't strong enough yet for this particular exercise and should be established first.
3. **Mountain climbers**: A dynamic exercise that not only targets the lower abs but also increases heart rate, improving cardiovascular fitness.

4. **Reverse Crunches**: Lift your hips off the floor and bring your knees towards your chest, which emphasises lower abdominal engagement.
5. **Planks with leg lifts**: Performing a plank and alternately lifting each leg puts more emphasis on the lower abs and the core stability muscles.
6. **V-ups**: From a lying position, lift your legs and torso simultaneously, try to touch your toes, to intensely work the lower abs.
7. **Scissor kicks**: Lie on your back and alternate leg lifts in a scissor motion to engage the lower abdominals and increase core endurance.
8. **Flutter kicks:** Like scissor kicks, but with a smaller range of motion and faster pace, flutter kicks intensely target the lower abs.
9. **Russian twists with leg raise:** Adding a leg raise to the Russian twist not only works the obliques, but also puts focus on the lower abdominal region.
10. **Ab rollouts:** Using an ab wheel or a barbell, roll out from a kneeling position to full extension and back, this engages the whole core, including the lower abs.

> Clinical Tip: Incorporating these exercises into your routine will help build strength in the lower abdominals. It's crucial to perform them with proper form to maximise effectiveness and reduce the risk of injury. Additionally, for best results, combine these exercises with overall core strengthening, cardio, and a healthy diet to reduce body fat and make the lower abdominal muscles more visible.

Contact us directly to get these in video format.

SEVEN-DAY RIDER FITNESS AND CORE CONDITIONING PLAN (14 YRO+)

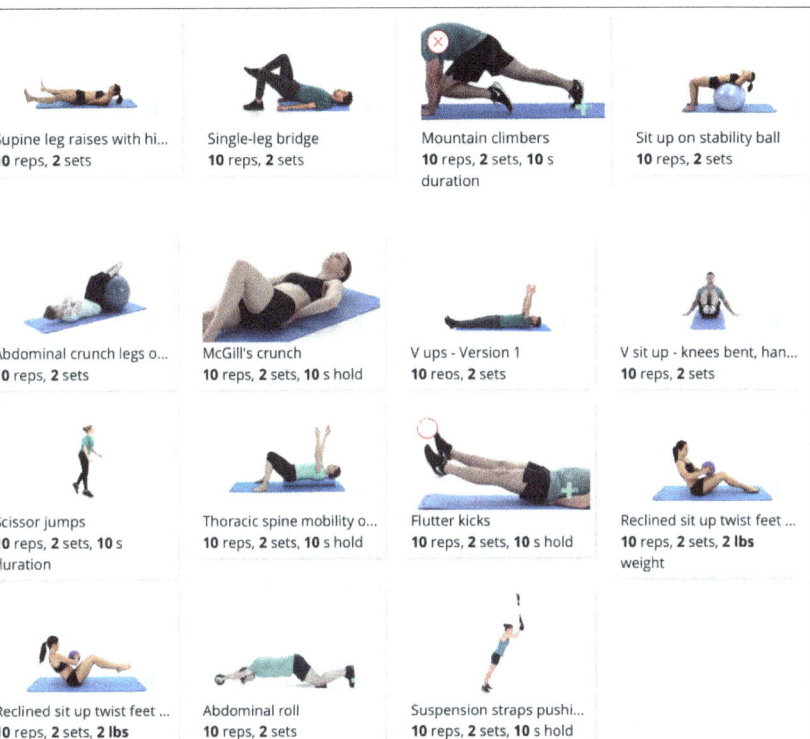

A 7-DAY RIDER MUSCLE STRENGTHENING PROGRAMME EXAMPLE

(WEEK 3 WOULD CHANGE TO 4 X 8 REPS)

Day 1: Lower Body Strength
Squats: 3 sets of 8-12 reps
Lunges: 3 sets of 8-12 reps per leg
Romanian deadlifts: 3 sets of 8-12 reps

Calf raises: 3 sets of 15 reps
Step-ups: 3 x 10 reps
Cable pull through: 2 x 10 reps
Kettlebell swings: 2 x 10 reps

Day 2: Upper Body Strength
Push-ups: 3 sets of 8-12 reps
Dumbbell rows: 3 sets of 8-12 reps per arm
Plank to push-up: 3 sets of 8 reps
Bicep curls: 3 sets of 12 reps
Dart: 2 x 10 reps (10 sec holds)
Prone superman: 2 x 10 reps

Day 3: Core and Stability
Planks: 3 sets of 30-60 seconds
Side planks: 3 sets of 30 seconds per side
Russian twists: 2 sets of 10 reps per side
Bird dogs: 2 sets of 12 reps per side

Day 4: Active Recovery
Light cycling or swimming for 30-45 minutes, focus on maintaining a low intensity to aid recovery and improve endurance without impacting strength gains significantly.

Day 5: Flexibility and Balance
Yoga or Pilates session focused on flexibility, core strength and balance, essential for riding.

Day 6: High-Intensity Interval Training (HIIT)
20-minute HIIT session including exercises like kettlebell swings, box jumps and burpees, aimed at improving power

and cardiovascular health. Incorporate short, intense bursts of activity followed by brief rest periods.

Day 7: Rest
Complete rest or gentle stretching for recovery and muscle repair, preparing for next week.

This workout plan blends resistance training with endurance, flexibility and recovery activities to build strength, improve balance and enhance cardiovascular health, directly supporting the needs of horse riders. Remember, it's crucial to adjust the intensity, volume and frequency of these workouts to match your current fitness level and riding goals and consider consulting a fitness professional to tailor the programme further to your needs.

CHAPTER 17

WHAT ABOUT THE HORSE? COMMON INJURIES AFTER A FALL

If your horse has also fallen with the rider, please get them checked ASAP by a fully qualified medical professional like a Chiropractor, ACPAT physiotherapist or Equine specific vet. Check the RAMP register, which highlights the best in the field in musculoskeletal animal practitioners, in your local area.
https://www.rampregister.org

It is vitally important to check for fractures, especially on the hips and pelvis after a side fall. These are usually most apparent in cross country events.

After a fall, horses can sustain a variety of injuries, with the severity and type often depending on factors such as the nature of the fall, the landing surface and the activity being performed at the time. Common injuries include:

Soft Tissue Injuries: Sprains, strains and bruises are prevalent, affecting muscles, ligaments and tendons. These can occur anywhere on the body but are particularly common in the legs and back, where stress from the fall is often absorbed.

Cuts and Abrasions: Falls can lead to various degrees of skin damage, from minor scrapes to deep lacerations, especially when the horse falls on rough or uneven surfaces.

Joint Injuries: The impact of a fall can lead to joint injuries such as dislocations or articular fractures, particularly in the knees, hocks and fetlocks, where the force of impact is often concentrated.

Bone Fractures: More severe falls can result in fractures, ranging from simple cracks to compound fractures requiring immediate veterinary intervention. Legs and ribs are common sites for fractures, but the severity and location can vary widely.

Head and Neck Injuries: Falls can cause trauma to the head and neck area, leading to concussions, dental injuries or even more severe conditions like cervical vertebral instability (often referred to as "wobbler syndrome").

Spinal Injuries: Though less common, serious falls can lead to spinal injuries, which can be particularly concerning due to the potential for permanent damage and impairment.

Internal Injuries: Impact with obstacles or a hard landing can cause internal injuries, including bruising or rupture of internal organs, internal bleeding or damage to the respiratory system.

Preventing injuries involves proper training, conditioning and use of protective gear like boots and wraps for the horse. Regular veterinary check-ups can also help identify and mitigate potential health issues that could increase the risk of falls or injury. After a fall, it's crucial to assess the horse for injuries thoroughly and consult a veterinarian immediately if any injuries are suspected, ensuring the best possible outcome for the horse's recovery.

Many showjumping horses experience issues with their suspensory ligaments. The stresses placed on the hindlimb suspensory apparatus (on take-off) and the forelimb suspensory apparatus (on landing) put enormous strain on these important ligaments. The hind limbs provide most of the force for take-off, and the head and neck position changes to ensure optimal force generation.

On landing, the front coffin and fetlock joints are overextended (hyperextended) which places strain on the flexor tendons and the suspensory ligaments in these limbs. It is not therefore surprising that damage to these ligaments and tendons can be commonly found in showjumping horses which will lead to lameness and a period of rest and recuperation, including splint injuries.

SJ and XC horses are particularly susceptible to fetlock and shoulder and lower cervical spine impacts, as well as hock and stifle issues which are especially common. Dressage horses tend to have hocks and HL issues like DDFT and suspension ligament injuries including sacroiliac joint inflammation.

Now that you understand ground reaction forces and its impacts, hopefully this should make more sense.

Clinical Tip: Consider incorporating regular bodywork sessions, such as massage or chiropractic treatments, to help maintain the horse's overall muscular and skeletal health. Consult with professionals experienced in equine physical therapy to develop a tailored programme that addresses any specific areas of concern. Also, consider the therapies we discuss in the section below as options for strength training and event preparation.

CHAPTER 18

WOUND REPAIR AND TISSUE HEALING HACKS

The picture below represents the stages of wound repair from homeostasis to wound contraction.

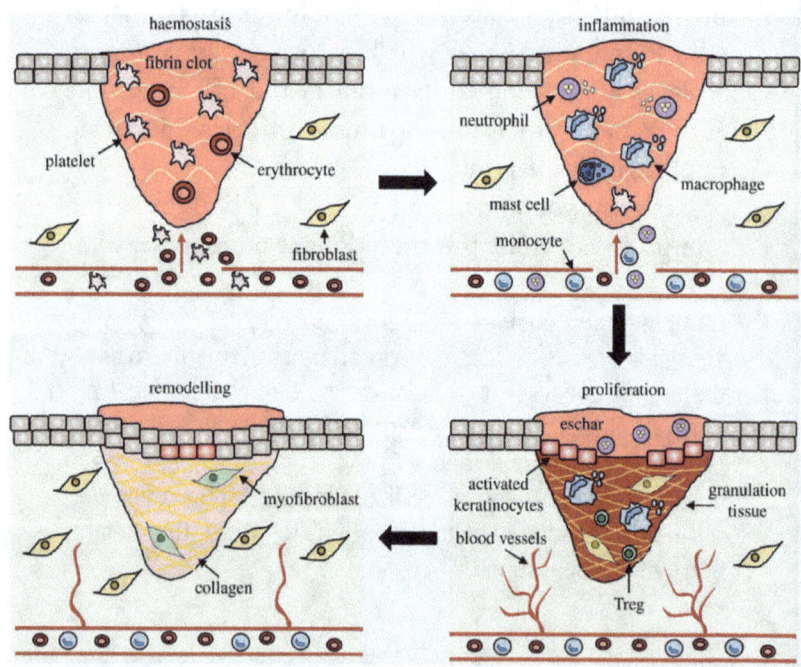

WHEN WOUNDS DON'T HEAL

The process of acute wound repair involves a complex series of cellular signals and behaviours aimed at swiftly closing the skin barrier. However, when this process fails to occur properly, it can result in excessive scarring or failure to heal altogether, leading to the development of chronic wounds which persist beyond 12 weeks.

In mammals, ageing and diabetes contribute to the gradual loss of dermal matrix, altering tissue mechanics, reducing resilience and increasing susceptibility to friction damage. Human tissue healing follows a well-defined timeline. Initially, immediate responses such as clotting aim to stop bleeding and cover the open wound. The granulation phase, occurring within the first few days up to four weeks post-injury (depending on wound size), involves tissue regeneration. The subsequent re-epithelialisation phase sees new skin attempting to grow and cover the wound site. However, the formation of "proud flesh", or excessive granulation tissue, can disrupt normal tissue regrowth. Healing may take up to 12 months to complete fully.

Early intervention by a skilled equine medical practitioner utilising scar-work therapy and laser therapy has been shown to regulate tissue growth and prevent the buildup of fascial adhesions over injured sites, thereby facilitating long-term tissue recovery and function.

CHAPTER 19
THE FOUNDATIONS OF RIDER FITNESS, BALANCE AND BIOMECHANICS

A significant portion of riders and coaches dedicate their efforts to enhancing their horses' movement and carriage. However, achieving the desired harmony and unity in riding can greatly benefit from riders prioritising their own balance, flexibility and strength. Beyond just being physically fit to ride, riders should adopt a defensive riding approach and possess basic skills to handle potential dangers. Fitness serves as a formidable defence against injuries, as it enhances reaction time, balance and agility.

An effective strength training routine for equestrians should incorporate a blend of compound lifts and isolated exercises. Compound lifts like deadlifts and squats engage multiple muscle groups simultaneously, fostering overall strength development. However, as riders, we must also prioritise precise and independent aids without undue tension or

imbalance. This necessitates isolating individual muscle groups while maintaining a stable yet supple core.

Isolated and unilateral exercises are invaluable in this regard. Movements such as single-leg deadlifts, leg presses, rows and calf raises target specific muscle groups essential for riding. By honing these muscles, riders can enhance their posture, control and communication with the horse, thereby refining their riding technique.

Core stability is another cornerstone of equestrian fitness. While traditional core exercises like crunches and planks have their merits, they may fall short in meeting the demands of riding. Riders must uphold trunk stability while dynamically coordinating limb movements to convey precise cues to the horse.

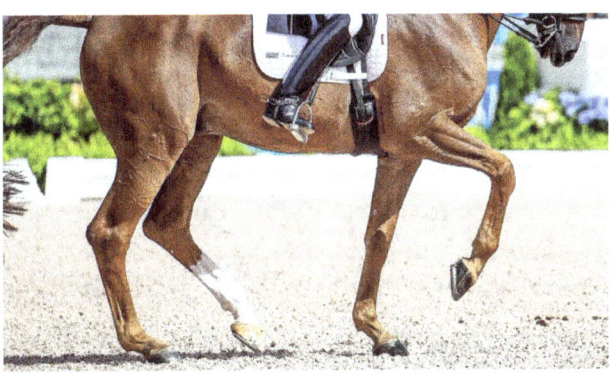

For instance, executing an isolated half-halt aid with one arm while applying pressure with the opposite leg to prompt the horse to bend through a corner requires precise muscle activation and trunk stability. Incorporating exercises that mimic these movements, such as high plank with shoulder taps, suitcase carry marches and bear crawls, can bolster core stability and enhance the rider's ability to manage isolated limb movement while in the saddle.

Collapsing in the saddle, as opposed to maintaining a straight, aligned posture, can have several negative effects on both the horse and rider within the context of horse riding. Good posture is crucial in riding for balance, effective communication and overall performance. Here's how collapsing in the saddle can be detrimental:

FOR THE RIDER

Compromised Balance: A rider who collapses in the saddle—leaning too far forward, slumping or tilting—can throw off their balance. This makes it harder to ride effectively, especially during manoeuvres that require precise weight distribution.

Increased Risk of Injury: Poor posture increases the risk of injury in the event of a fall, as the rider may not be positioned to roll or absorb impact safely. Additionally, repetitive strain from poor posture can lead to back, neck and shoulder injuries over time.

Reduced Effectiveness of Aids: Aids (signals communicated to the horse via leg, seat and hand cues) can become unclear or inconsistent if a rider's posture is compromised. This can lead to confusion for the horse and hinder its performance.

Fatigue: Collapsing instead of sitting straight can lead to quicker onset of fatigue due to inefficient use of muscles. Proper alignment allows for better use of core muscles, reducing the effort needed to maintain position.

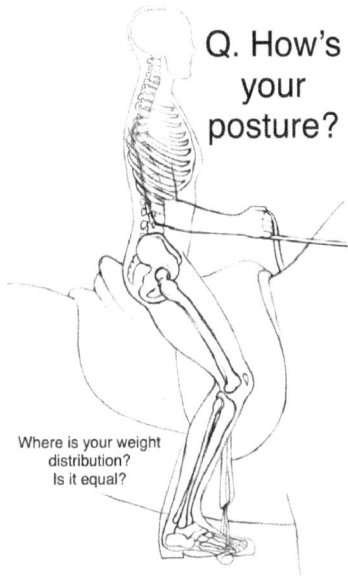

IMPROVING POSTURE

Correcting posture in the saddle involves:
- Awareness of one's own posture and alignment
- Regular exercises to strengthen the core and improve balance
- Lessons with a qualified instructor to correct bad habits and develop proper riding techniques
- Using equipment that is properly fitted for both horse and rider, ensuring comfort and facilitating correct posture

Maintaining a straight, aligned posture while riding not only enhances the effectiveness and safety of the rider but also ensures the well-being and performance of the horse.

FOR THE HORSE

Discomfort and Pain: A rider who collapses can inadvertently apply uneven pressure on the horse's back, leading to discomfort or even pain. Over time, this can cause physical issues for the horse, including back soreness or more serious musculoskeletal problems.

Impaired Performance: The horse's ability to perform certain movements or manoeuvres can be significantly hampered by a rider's poor posture. Balance and rhythm, essential for disciplines such as dressage, jumping, and reining, can be negatively affected.

Behavioural Issues: Horses may develop behavioural issues as a response to the discomfort or confusion caused by a rider's poor posture. These issues can manifest as reluctance to move forward, difficulty in executing commands, or even resistance and bucking.

Training and Communication Problems: Effective communication between horse and rider is a foundation of successful riding. A rider's collapsed posture can lead to miscommunications, making training more difficult and potentially reinforcing incorrect responses in the horse.

It should be the responsibility of the owner and rider to make sure that both parties are fit enough and symmetrical enough for the tasks asked of the horse.

Nutrition plays a major role in sports performance, as does an appropriate training schedule. Please ask your qualified rehabilitative therapist to help design a tailor-made plan for you and your horse.

This should take into account the past year's successes and challenges. Including preventative work for stability and strengthening after an injury.

Do not throw yourself into competition life again quickly after a break, unless you have had some refresher lessons with a qualified instructor, capable of helping you progress in your chosen discipline. Also, assuming you have already had your horse and your body checked and corrected for any underlying issues.

30-Day Rider Fitness Plan

Week 1: Foundation Building
Day 1: Yoga for flexibility: Focus on yoga poses that enhance flexibility and core stability, such as the plank, warrior III and downward dog.
Day 2: Pilates basics: Emphasis on core engagement through exercises like the hundred, single leg stretches and criss-cross.
Day 3: Rest or light swimming: Engage in light swimming activities focusing on freestyle or breaststroke to enhance core stability without overexerting, ideally 30-45 minutes.
Day 4: Weight training fundamentals: Focus on basic weight training exercises targeting the back and abdominal muscles. Include deadlifts, squats and lunges with light weights.
Day 5: CrossFit intro: Focus on exercises that improve core stability and strength. Include air squats, burpees and sit-ups.
Day 6: Balance and proprioceptive training: Use balance boards or stability balls for exercises that challenge balance and enhance proprioception.
Day 7: Rest

Week 2: Building Strength and Stability
Day 8-14: Repeat Week 1 schedule, gradually increasing the intensity of each session. Add more challenging poses in yoga and Pilates, increase weights during weight training, incorporate longer swimming sessions and add more repetitions or sets in CrossFit.

Week 3: Intensification and Integration
Day 15-21: Continue the rotation, focusing on integrating exercises from different disciplines.

Combine yoga and Pilates sessions to enhance both flexibility and core strength.

Integrate balance and proprioceptive exercises into weight training sessions by using stability balls or balance boards.

Increase CrossFit intensity with exercises that require greater core engagement, such as kettlebell swings and wall balls.

Incorporate endurance swimming sessions focusing on core engagement throughout.

Week 4: Peak and Maintenance
Day 22-28: This week, focus on reaching peak intensity while maintaining a balance across activities.

Introduce advanced yoga and Pilates poses that challenge core stability and flexibility.

Incorporate compound weightlifting movements, such as the clean and jerk, which require significant core engagement.

Increase CrossFit intensity with challenging workouts that focus on core strength.

Include longer and more intense swimming sessions, using techniques that challenge core stability and endurance.

Day 29:   Rest or active recovery: Engage in light activities such as walking or gentle yoga to aid recovery while keeping the body active.
Day 30:   Assess your progress in core stability, balance and overall fitness. Engage in a light activity of choice, focusing on enjoyment and relaxation.

Additional Notes:
- Ensure each workout begins with a warm-up and ends with a cool-down to prevent injuries.
- Listen to your body and adjust the intensity of workouts as needed.
- Incorporate rest days to allow for recovery and muscle growth.
- Consult with a fitness professional to ensure exercises are performed correctly and to adjust the plan according to personal fitness levels and goals.

RIDE STRONG: CORE CONDITIONING FOR EQUESTRIANS

Pilates and yoga are excellent for riders to enhance the foundations of "core" stability, balance and endurance. Some of our favourite recommendations are regarding the relationship between abdominal control, diaphragmatic breathing and hip stability for riders. We will cover the details of this in our next book for riders called "Beyond the Reins: Exploring the Neurological Foundations of Rider Performance".

Here are a few basic exercises to get you started.

Ideally balance exercises for horse riders would be completed every day after a fall, for eight weeks. Then balance exercises should be incorporated three times a week into a normal training regime.

Research suggests a 45-minute balance specific workout twice a week for healthy equestrians. (Brahman et al, 2017)

When I worked in professional sports, our athletes would train for 10-15 hours each week then practise mindfulness drills at home. The research showed that players who visualised the movements needed to get the goal/dunk the hoop, etc. would be more successful than the players who did the physical training.

Endurance athletes complete one-three hours of training daily in their sports, broken into sections with muscle recovery massage, chiropractic work and cryotherapy to finish.

VIP MUSCLES FOR RIDERS

The most important muscle groups to keep strong symmetrically for horse riders include:

- Lumbar paraspinals called multifidus and the erector spinae
- Back rotators like quadratus lumborum and the obliques
- Hip stabilisers like gluteus Medius and the abductors like TFL which tend to be underdeveloped in riders, and the adductors which tend to be overused on riders that grip their knees into the saddle.

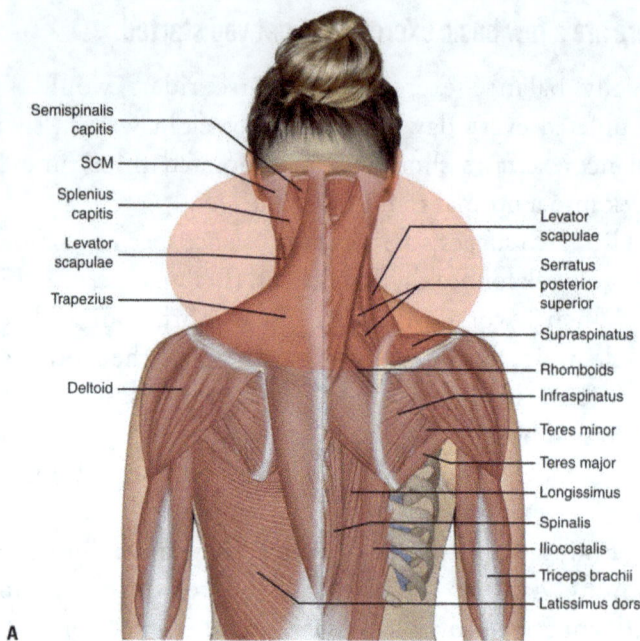

- Hip extensors like the gluteus maximus which are often weak in people who have desk jobs or have had previous horse riding falls, and the hamstrings which, more often than not, are too tight.
- Abdominals and back muscles should ideally always be working together, but commonly in riders we see the back working extra hard and glutes and abdominals failing to hold any kind of endurance required for stability.
- Pectoral chest muscles are often short in riders and especially in people with a manual job and horses at home. Rounded, forward drawn shoulders are typical of desk postures but to the detriment of mid back (thoracic) and scapular stabilisers.

THE FOUNDATIONS OF RIDER FITNESS, BALANCE AND BIOMECHANICS | 149

- Hip flexors like iliopsoas which actually attaches from the back of your spine to the front of your hip and into your diaphragm.

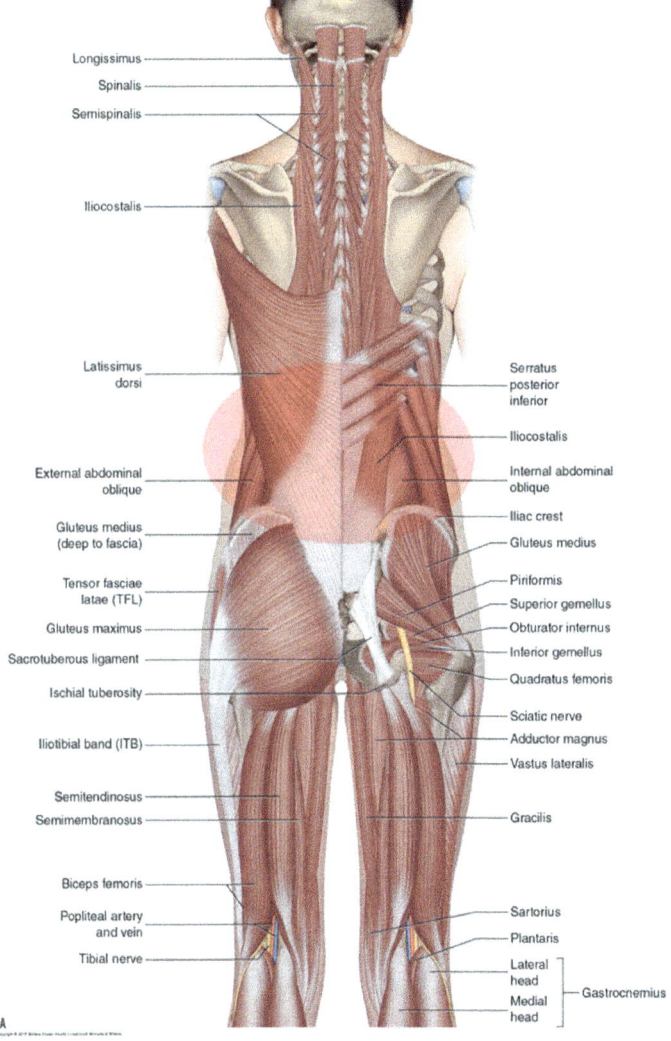

Therefore, if your instructors are often telling you that your shoulders are too far forward, you're not rotating through your spine enough or you're leaning in the saddle, then an underlying weakness, asymmetry in your body mechanics and /or postural pattern will need to be addressed. Just them shouting at you to make a change in the neurology behind these faulty movement patterns will make zero difference long term at all.

Also how do you tell if it's you or the horse that's crooked?? More on that in our next book.

CHAPTER 20

SMART RECOVERY – HOW TO USE NEUROSCIENCE AND CELL BIOLOGY TO REDUCE RECOVERY TIMES

CAN FALLS BE PREVENTED AND RECOVERY ACCELERATED?

Tissue recovery times can indeed be shortened by finding the right practitioner, with the right tools, at the right time.

Human tissue recovery times vary depending on factors such as the type and severity of the injury, individual health status and the body's natural healing processes. However, there are general timelines and scientific principles behind tissue healing.

The Inflammatory Phase: This initial stage of healing begins immediately after injury and lasts for a few days. It involves the release of inflammatory mediators, such as cytokines and growth factors, which attract immune cells to the site of injury. These immune cells remove debris and foreign substances, control bleeding and initiate the repair process.

The Proliferative Phase: Following the inflammatory phase, the proliferative phase begins, typically lasting

Average tissue healing time & factors which influence normal Recovery

MUSCLE STRAIN	Grade 1 Grade 2 Grade 3	2-8 weeks 2-4 months 9-12 months
TENDON INJURY	Acute Subacute Chronic Tear, rupture or repair	2-6 weeks 2-4 months 3-9 months 4-12+ months
LIGAMENT INJURY	Grade 1 Grade 2 Grade 3 Graft (Surgery)	2-8 weeks 2-6 months 6-12 months 12+ months
OTHER TISSUE	Bone Fracture Articular Cartilage Meniscus Labrum Nerves	6-12 weeks 9-24 months 3-12 months 2-5 years

THESE TIMELINES ARE GENERAL GUIDELINES, MANY TISSUES STILL CONTINUE TO SHOW EVIDENCE OF REMODELING AND MATURATION FOR 1-2 YEARS AFTER AN INJURY.

FACTORS INFLUENCING TISSUE HEALING TIMES

- Body Mechanics: Improving faulty mechanics to offload affected tissues
- Tissue Loading: No overloading, appropriate loading to drive an improved healing response. A tailor-made exercise plan is key that is adapted appropriately as you heal.
- Hydration: Well hydrated tissues heal faster.
- Nutrition: Protein requirements are increased in healing tissue.
- Sleep/Recovery Sleep depth/quality is more important than sleep quantity. Better sleep improves cellular repair & reduces excessive inflammation

from a few days to several weeks. During this phase, fibroblasts migrate to the injury site and start producing collagen, the main structural protein in connective tissues. Angiogenesis, the formation of new blood vessels, also occurs to supply oxygen and nutrients to the healing tissue. Granulation tissue, composed of collagen, blood vessels and inflammatory cells fill the wound and provide a scaffold for tissue repair.

The Remodelling Phase: The remodelling phase begins around three weeks after the injury and can continue for several months or even years. During this phase, collagen fibres reorganise and realign to strengthen the tissue, making it more resilient. The goal is to restore the tissue's structure and function as closely as possible to its pre-injury state.

THE FIVE BIGGEST FACTORS THAT INFLUENCE TISSUE HEALING

Nutrition: Adequate intake of nutrients such as protein, vitamins (e.g. vitamin C, which is essential for collagen synthesis) and minerals (e.g. zinc) is crucial for tissue repair.

Blood Supply: Proper blood flow to the injured area is essential for delivering oxygen and nutrients and removing waste products.

Immune Response: An appropriate inflammatory response is necessary to initiate healing, but excessive inflammation can delay or impair tissue repair.

Mechanical Factors: Proper immobilisation or support of the injured area can promote healing, while excessive stress or movement may hinder it.

Age: Tissue healing tends to be slower in older individuals due to age-related changes in cell function and decreased regenerative capacity.

> **Clinical Tip:** Understanding the science behind tissue healing can guide treatment strategies to optimise recovery and promote optimal outcomes.

CHAPTER 21

BALANCE AND THE BRAIN – THE SCIENCE OF LEARNING AND ADAPTATION

Our nervous system responds and learns by a process called neuroplasticity.

Neural plasticity, also known as brain plasticity, is the brain's ability to reorganise itself by forming new neural connections throughout life. This process plays a crucial role in learning and memory formation, including the acquisition of skills to prevent injuries.

When individuals engage in activities aimed at injury prevention, such as proper form during exercise or using ergonomic techniques in daily tasks, neural plasticity comes into play. Through repeated practice and reinforcement, the brain forms new neural pathways associated with these preventive behaviours.

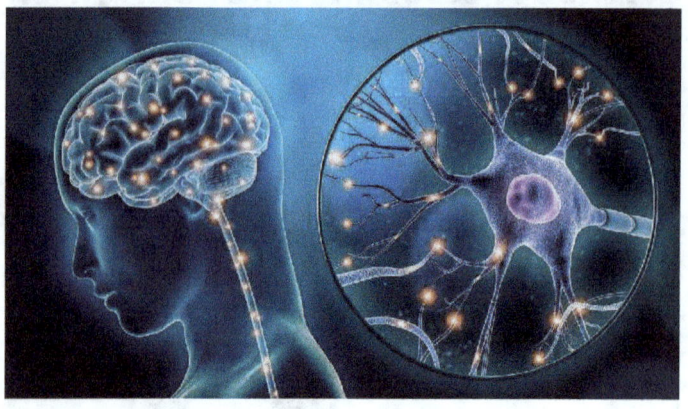

For example, when learning correct lifting techniques to avoid back injuries, the brain undergoes changes in the structure and function of relevant neural circuits. With continued practice, these neural pathways become more efficient and automatic, reducing the risk of injury. Additionally, feedback mechanisms, such as proprioception (the sense of body position), contribute to the refinement of motor skills and coordination, further enhancing injury prevention.

The nerves and the brain have the capacity to change their connections and behaviour in response to new information, sensory stimulus development, damage or dysfunction.

Although some nervous system functions appear to be hard-wired into our system, specific localised regions of our brain and certain nerve networks have shown the ability to modulate and carry out specific functions while at the same time, retaining the capacity to deviate from their usual job.

Neuroplasticity is a very complex multifaceted fundamental property of our brain. Our brain also has the ability to divert its attention and strengthen pathways that we need on a regular basis. For example, once you have learned to ride a bike, you don't have to keep relearning it again and again. Your brain has understood that this pathway was important to you and made it a strong connection.

Neuroplasticity is used by the brain during the reinforcement of sensory information through experience, such as learning something new and memory, but also following actual physical damage to the brain when the brain attempts to compensate for lost activity.

The largest amount of developmental plasticity occurs in the first few years of life, when our neurons grow very rapidly and send out multiple branches, forming millions of connections. By the age of three, we have around 15,000 connections called synapses for every neuron. As an adult, our connections would be around half that number, because the nervous system will break away any connections that are not reinforced. In other words, the brain trims back anything it doesn't think is useful.

Overall, neural plasticity enables the brain to adapt and learn from experiences, allowing individuals to acquire and refine injury prevention strategies, ultimately promoting safer and healthier behaviours.

BALANCE AND FALLS PREVENTION

Strength training builds strong muscles, which are the foundation for preventing falls. Balance exercises can build on this foundation to make training more specific and effective in further decreasing the risk of falling with more functional, task-specific exercises.

Neurologically speaking, balance is a multifaceted process including your ankle and foot stability and mechanics, your vision (visual processing systems through your eyes and cranial nerves 2,3,4 & 6, pons and occipital lobes of your brain), your inner ear (vestibular system) and your cerebellum (the part of your brain that coordinates movement and awareness called proprioception).

The cerebellum (meaning little brain in Latin), fine tunes motor activity or movement, e.g. the fine movements of your fingers as they perform surgery or paint a picture. It helps us maintain posture and our sense of balance or equilibrium, by controlling the tone of muscles and the position of limbs. The cerebellum is important in your ability to perform rapid and repetitive actions such as playing a video game. In the cerebellum, right-sided abnormalities produce symptoms on the same side of the body.

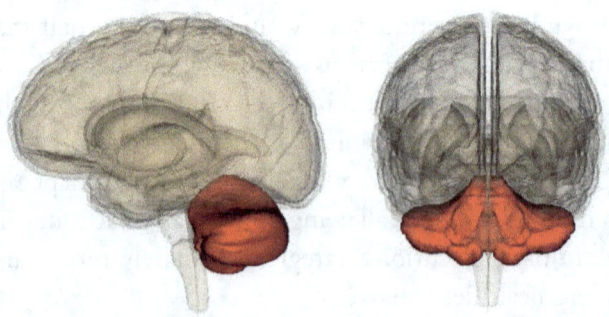

The Cerebellum is depicted in this image of a human brain in red. The picture on the left is a transverse section of the human brain (cut in half), the picture on the right is a view from behind (back of your skull).

The cerebellum comprises small lobes and serves several functions.
- It receives information from the inner ear's balance system, sensory nerves, auditory and visual systems. It is involved in the coordination of movements and motor learning.
- It is associated with motor movement and control, but this is not because the motor commands originate here. Instead, the cerebellum modifies these signals and makes motor movements accurate and useful.
- It helps control posture, balance and the coordination of voluntary movements. This allows different muscle groups to act together and produce coordinated fluid movement.
- In addition to playing an essential role in motor control, the cerebellum is also important in certain cognitive functions, including speech.

The pons is a different region of the brainstem located above the medulla oblongata and below the midbrain. While the primary function of the pons is to serve as a relay centre for signals travelling between different parts of the brain, it also plays a role in vision.

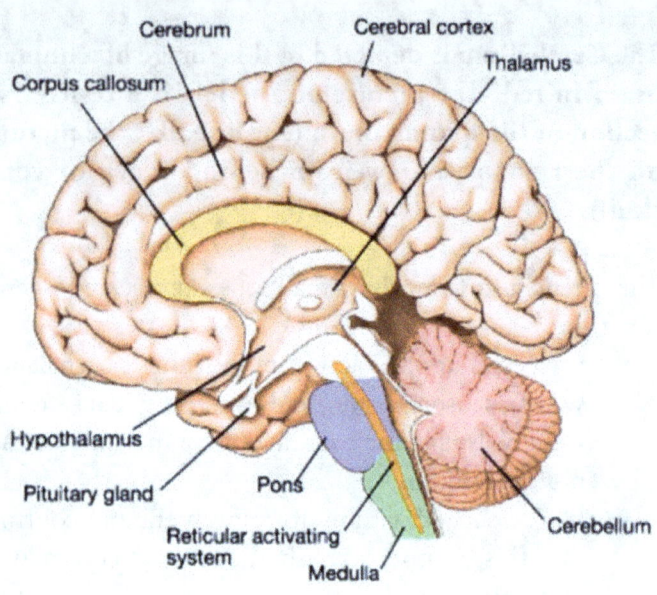

The pons in this image is a transverse cut of the human brain, depicted in purple.

Specifically, the pons contains nuclei that are involved in the control of eye movements and coordination. These nuclei receive input from various parts of the brain, including the visual cortex, and help regulate the movement of the eyes to ensure smooth and coordinated tracking of objects in the visual field. Additionally, the pons is connected to other brain regions involved in visual processing, such as the superior colliculus and the cerebellum, further contributing to its role in vision. Overall, while the pons is primarily associated with functions such as breathing, sleep and arousal, its involvement in coordinating eye movement underscores its significance in visual perception and control.

CAN I RETRAIN MY BRAIN?

Neuroplasticity programmes typically involve a combination of visualisation, meditation, breath work and behavioural exercises. Using brain retraining that involves your limbic system, it is possible to calm down the nervous system which has become overly sensitive and/or overly responsive to certain triggers even after they've stopped being harmful or useful. The goal is to rewire the neural pathways and reprogramme the responses that might be keeping your body stuck and not moving forward into balance.

CHAPTER 22
BRAIN-RETRAINING: FOUNDATIONAL BALANCE EXERCISE HOMEWORK

Clinical Tip: Before starting any new exercise programme, please get a check-up by a neurology specific Chiropractor or qualified Physiotherapist. This will ensure that exercises are appropriate, and that no underlying issues need to be addressed before you begin.

EXERCISE 1

Standing with your eyes open initially.

Feet should be shoulder width apart initially. Then get narrower.

stay steady for 30 seconds.

No sway, ankle wobbling or leaning forward, backward or sideways

Wear properly supported trainers

Feet apart: Stand with feet about shoulder-width apart, eyes open, and hold steady for ten seconds, working your way up to 30 seconds. This may take only a few attempts to master, depending on your current nervous system health.

If you find yourself swaying or reaching for the wall or counter frequently, just keep working on this exercise until you can do it with minimal swaying or support. Once you can hold this position firmly for 30 seconds, move on to the next exercise. If, however, this is still not possible after one week, then please see a professional that understands neurology to test you more.

Feet together: Stand with feet together, eyes open, and hold steady for ten seconds, working your way up to 30 seconds over seven days. Once you can do this exercise for 30 seconds with minimal swaying or support, move on to the next one.

Feet together and eyes shut: Ideally 15 seconds is what would be normal for people under 50, without balance disorders, a new whiplash injury or diabetes. Work towards this by holding your fingers against the wall in front of you and then take your hands off the wall over time. If you are struggling to stand still for even a few seconds, have your medical professional check for vestibular disorders or inner ear conditions before continuing.

One leg stands (stand on one foot) eyes open: Hold steady for ten seconds, working up to 30 seconds. Switch to the other foot and repeat three times daily for two weeks. Do not drop your opposite hip when standing on one leg or lean to the side. Try to focus to keep your weight evenly distributed on your standing leg. Don't rest your leg on your knee; that's cheating!

One leg stand eyes open. Keep your weight evenly distributed on your stance foot. (Like standing on 3 points of a triangle (big toe, little toe, heel).

One leg stands and eyes closed: Only complete this exercise once you can perform the previous exercises safely and with little or no support. Hold for five seconds, working up to 30 seconds over two weeks.

The goal for each exercise is to hold the position for ten seconds and progress to 30 seconds, five repetitions (including five per leg on the one-foot exercises), three times daily.

EXERCISE PROGRESSIONS FOR PEOPLE WHO LIKE TO MOVE UP QUICKLY

- One leg stand, eyes open on a balance pad. Then on a wobble board. Then with trainers on and off. Then on pad while bouncing a large Pilates ball off the wall and catching it.

- The one leg stands, eyes open while turning your head ten degrees left and right and repeat ten times.
- Then one leg stands, eyes open in a balance board while counting back from 30 in threes.
- Then one leg stands, eyes open on a wobble board while naming the months of the year and only saying every second one aloud.
- Then one leg stands into a single leg squat. Especially with arms out in front to reach the body weight forward. Remember your knee should not come over the top of your foot here.
- Then one leg stands while reaching for something in front of you. We like to use cones placed in front of our patients in an arc in the floor and they have to reach to touch a tennis ball in sequence in the top of each cone.

Pictures above: one leg stand hip airplanes.

- Then one leg stands into a dynamic movement pattern such as into a knee raise and then with a leg swing.
- One leg stands with arm punches using a dumbbell.
- Hip hinge from a single leg stance into an airplane stance. Reach your arms out to the side to form a T-shape with your body.

> CONGRATULATIONS – you got through all the anatomy and neuroscience unscathed!

CHAPTER 23

A SNEAK PEAK – HOW TO RECOVER QUICKLY AND EFFECTIVELY

Now that you know all the secrets of tissue healing, the latest research on what treatment modalities is recommended most and the anatomy involved in the recovery process, it will be easy for you to guess my cheat sheet for recovery post-fall.

> **My Diagnosis: SIJ and lumbar spine facet sprain and L5 nerve root irritation**

EXAMPLE 1: 30-DAY RIDER RECOVERY PLAN FOR ACUTE LOW BACK AND SIJ SPRAIN

Week 1 Daily Routine
- Sit on upright seats like dining chairs only for 30 minutes at a time.
- Use crutches for walking for first three days to reduce load on inflamed joints.
- Hot water bottle over lumbosacral junction three times daily for 15 minutes maximum for direct pain relief

- Pillow between the knees when sleeping, lying in unaffected side. Bolster with pillows behind to support lumbar spine.
- Vinyasa Yoga for 20 minutes, focus on back-strengthening poses like downward dog with leg extension, child's pose, plank and warrior poses.
- Perform hamstring stretches after the yoga session to ensure flexibility and reduce the risk of injury after a lower back impact. Nerve tension will feel like tugging in the hamstring so take it slow. If you have any pins and needles on hamstring stretches, stop and adapt to seated nerve mobilisations instead. Three times ten seconds each side.
- Twenty times pelvic tilts and upper thoracic independent motion in rotation for lumbar spine and pelvis. Seated and lying with your face upwards.
- Piriformis stretches seated with a tennis ball on the muscle and also lying supine (on your back with your face up) with one knee across the other. Three times ten-second holds on both sides (bilaterally).
- Cat stretches two times ten daily for five seconds. Arching and dipping lower back and pelvis only, while mid thoracic spine stays straight and stable like a tabletop.
- Hot tub five minutes daily at 38 degrees, while stretching the lower back in pelvic tilts.
- Cold water pod three minutes – full body immersion.
- Laser therapy 30 seconds constant with class 3B probe for pain relief. Laser cluster probe for

advanced tissue healing (2.5hz for two minutes over the source of inflammation).
- Kinesio taping of lumbar spine to support stabilisers.
- Acupuncture into the sacroiliac joint ligaments to reduce pain.
- Chiropractic joint manipulation and mobilisation on lumbar facet and sacroiliac joints (as tolerated initially), every two days for one week, then full spine ideally testing and adjusting to evaluate nervous system functionality and control.
- Ankle and foot joint manipulation for proprioceptive stimulation activity.

Week 2-4 Workout Schedule

Monday and Thursday (Strength Training)
- Warm-up: 15 minutes of light cardio (e.g. swimming or cycling)
- Deadlifts: 3 x 12 reps (initially with light weights, then progress)
- Seated cable row: 3 x 12 reps
- Shoulder press: 3 x 12 reps
- Squats: 3 x 12 reps
- Pelvic tilts into a bridge: 3 x 10 reps
- Single leg lift (while in bridge position): 2 x 20 reps per leg Lateral leg lifts for hip stability: 3 x 8 reps both sides
- Tricep dips, bicep curls and Lat pull downs: 3 x 10 reps bilaterally.
- Cool-down: 5 minutes of stretching yoga, focusing on the back, shoulders and gluteals

Tuesday and Friday (Balance and Proprioceptive Exercises)
- Warm-up: 10 minutes of light cardio on exercise bike
- Single-leg balance: 3 sets of 30 seconds per leg. Eyes open then with neck rotations
- Bosu ball squats: 3 sets of 8-12 reps
- Stability ball push-ups: 3 sets of 8-12 reps
- Hip Extensions with a TheraBand: 3 sets of 8-12 reps per leg
- Deadbug: 3 sets of 10-15 reps
- Cool-down: Piriformis and QL stretches

Wednesday (Rest or Light Activity)
- Optional light yoga focusing on relaxation and stretching poses
- Balance work standing on a pad, bosu ball, then wobble board. Trainers off and on to stimulate awareness
- Gentle seated twist, cat-cow stretch, supine twist, legs-up-the-wall pose

Saturday (Swimming and Sauna)
- Swimming: 30 minutes, focusing on different strokes
- Sauna: 15 minutes for relaxation
- Followed by a yoga session as described in the daily routine

Sunday (Active Recovery)
- A longer yoga session focusing on the poses listed in the daily routine plus additional Piriformis and QL stretches
- Pelvic tilts into a bridge and single leg lifts for a lower intensity focus on core and glute strength

This 30-day plan is designed to balance strength, flexibility and recovery, ensuring a holistic approach to fitness. Ideally you will work with a health professional who will adapt and change your routine every three weeks.

Clinical Tip: Ensure you perform hamstring stretches daily, ideally after the yoga session, to maintain flexibility.

Adjust the intensity of exercises based on your personal fitness level and pain tolerance. It's important to challenge yourself, but also to prevent over exertion. Nothing should increase your pain (the aim is to stabilise and calm things down).

Stay hydrated and maintain a balanced diet to support your exercise regimen. Turmeric and a good supplement with glucosamine, hyaluronic acid and MSM including Vitamin D3+ and K2 supplements for calcium metabolism.

Rest days are crucial for recovery. Ensure you're allowing your body to rest, especially if you're experiencing muscle soreness.

The equipment that would be useful at home would be:
- A thick yoga mat
- A pillow
- 2kg hand weight (bottle of water or tin of soup would do fine)
- A light and medium resistance band
- A balance pad
- A wobble board
- A beach towel

The inclusion of specific exercises like the deadbug, hip extensions with a TheraBand and piriformis and QL stretches, alongside daily yoga and hamstring stretches, targets core stability, lower back health and overall flexibility.

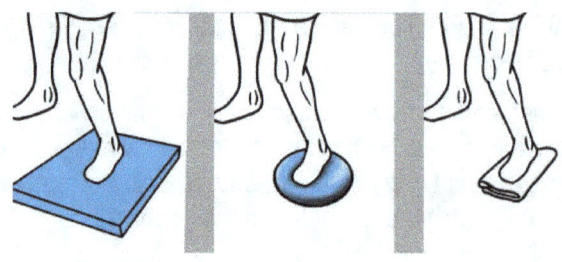

Phase 1: Foundation and Mobility (Weeks 1-4). Focus on gentle mobilisation, activation and foundational strength exercises. Prioritise pain-free movements.

Week 1-2: Mobility and Gentle Activation

Day 1, 3, 5: Mobility and Activation; Neck tilts and turns (for whiplash recovery): 2 sets of 10 reps. Shoulder blade squeezes: 2 sets of 15 reps. Wall angels: 10 reps. Pendulum exercises: 2 x 10 reps per arm

Day 2, 4: Thoracic Mobility; Cat-cow stretch: 2 x 15 reps. Thoracic rotations – 2 x 15 reps each side. Child's pose with side stretch – 10 reps, hold for 10-30 seconds each side, breath long and slow.

Week 3-4: Foundation Strengthening

Day 1, 3, 5: Shoulder Stability and Strength; Isometric shoulder external rotation: 2 sets of 10 seconds hold per side. Prone dart lifts – 2 x 10 reps each. Side-lying external rotation – 2 x 12 reps per arm.

Day 2, 4: Mid-Thoracic and Core Stability; Plank: 2 sets, 20 second hold. Side plank: 2 sets, 15 seconds hold per side. Deadbug: 2 x 15 reps per side.

Phase 2: Strengthening and Conditioning (Weeks 5-8) Introduce light weights and resistance bands to begin building strength.

Week 5-6: Introduction to Resistance

Day 1, 3, 5: Resistance Training; Band pull-apart: 3 x 15 reps. Dumbbell shoulder press (light weight):3 x 12 reps. Cervical rotation with hand (self resistance), 10 reps each side.

Day 2, 4: Mid-Thoracic Strengthening: Seated cable row (light resistance),3 x 12 reps. Supine thoracic extensions over foam roller, 3x10 reps. Birddogs, 3 x15 reps per side.

Week 7-8: Progressive Strengthening

Day 1, 3, 5: Progressive Shoulder and Back Strengthening; Increase weights for shoulder press: 3 sets of 10 reps. Lat pull downs: 3 x 12 reps. Single-arm dumbbell row: 3 x12 reps per side.

Day 2, 4: Enhanced Core and Thoracic Stability; Plank with arm lift: 3 x 10 reps per side. Side plank with rotation: 3 x10 reps per side. Half-kneeling chop and lift (with band): 3 x 12 reps per side.

Phase 3: Advanced Strengthening and Maintenance (Weeks 9-12) Focus on maintaining and enhancing the gains with increased resistance and complex movements.

Week 9-10: Advanced Resistance Training

Day 1, 3, 5: Advanced Shoulder Strengthening; Arnold press: 3 x 10 reps. Upright row with dumbbells 3 x 12 reps. Reverse flies with dumbbells 3 x12 reps.

Day 2, 4: Advanced Thoracic and Core Stability: Turkish get-up: 3 x 6 reps per side. Dynamic plank (plank to push-up position); 3 x 10 reps. Cable woodchopper: 3 x 12 reps per side.

Week 11-12: Maintenance and Functional Training
- Day 1, 3, 5: Shoulder and Core Functional Training
- Medicine ball slams: 3 x 15 reps
- Kettlebell swings: 3 x 15 reps
- TRX rows: 3 sets of 12 reps
- Day 2, 4: Mobility and Active Recovery
- Continue with mobility exercises from Weeks 1-2
- Yoga or Pilates for flexibility and core strength
- Light swimming (20-30 mins) or aqua therapy for non-impact conditioning

General Tips:
- Always warm-up before starting exercises and cool down afterwards.
- Gradually increase weights and resistance to avoid overloading the muscles.
- Ensure proper form and technique to prevent injuries.
- Consult with a professional trainer, especially when recovering from whiplash, to tailor the program to your specific needs and progress.

This structured program aims to build up shoulder and mid-thoracic stability and strength gradually, taking into account the recovery from whiplash and ensuring a comprehensive approach to physical wellness.

SPRAIN/STRAIN (WITHOUT TEAR) AND WHIPLASH Firstly, ensure that all your shoulder, elbow, wrist, mid thoracic spine and cervical neck joints are fully mobile and are no longer restricted.

RIB FRACTURES ARE ALL THEY ARE CRACKED UP TO BE

The only way to know for sure is to get it X-rayed. If you are suddenly short of breath after a fall and feel like you may have punctured a lung, then please go straight to A&E.

Telling the clinical difference between a punctured lung (pneumothorax) and a fractured rib can be complex because the symptoms can overlap, especially since a fractured rib can sometimes lead to a punctured lung. However, there are specific signs and symptoms for each condition that healthcare professionals use for diagnosis.

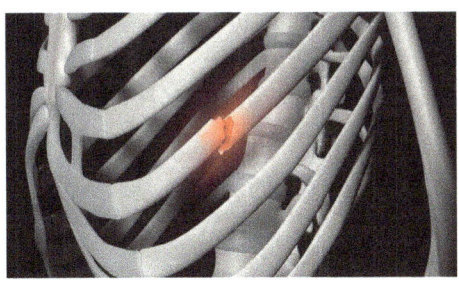

A FRACTURED RIB

- **Pain:** Sharp, severe pain at the site of the fracture. The pain usually worsens with deep breathing, coughing or movement.

- **Tenderness:** The area around the fractured rib is very tender to touch.
- **Swelling or Bruising:** Visible swelling or bruising may appear over the rib cage where the fracture has occurred.
- **Breathing Difficulty:** Although more commonly associated with a punctured lung, a fractured rib can also make it hard to take deep breaths due to pain.

Other injuries and how to deal with them

- **Sudden Chest Pain:** Sharp and sudden chest pain on one side that may worsen with deep breathing or coughing.
- **Shortness of Breath:** More pronounced difficulty breathing than with a fractured rib. This is due to air leaking into the space between the lung and chest wall, making it difficult for the lung to expand fully.
- **Rapid Heart Rate:** Increased heart rate as the body tries to compensate for the reduced oxygenation.
- **Cyanosis:** A bluish colour of the skin or lips due to lack of oxygen (in severe cases).
- **Fatigue:** Feeling tired or weak, also due to decreased oxygen supply.

If a lung collapses, then collapsed lung symptoms, in severe cases, may feel like the person is unable to catch their breath at all, indicating a collapsed portion of the lung.

Diagnosis? Healthcare professionals may use physical examination findings, the patient's history and imaging

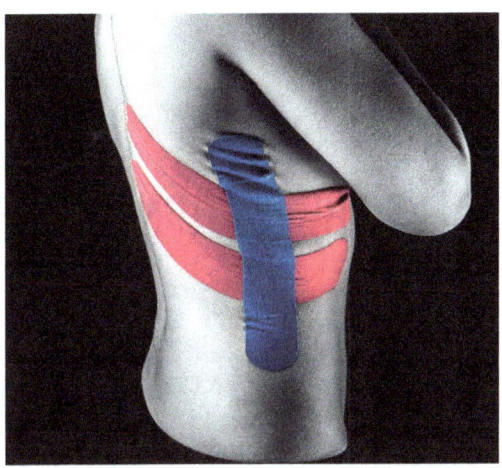

studies like X-rays or CT scans to differentiate between these conditions.

An X-ray can show both the presence of fractured ribs and whether there is air in the pleural space indicative of a pneumothorax.

Ask a professional to tape you up ASAP after a fall to help support your ribs while they heal. Ideally it should not have creases and folds like the image above as this will negatively affect your fascial and muscle tissue underneath.

It's very important to have the correct amount of tape tension and anchor points when applying sports tape. The quality of the tape should also be really high as the lower-level products have poor adhesive properties and can cause a rash.

> Clinical Tip: Both conditions are serious and require medical attention. A fractured rib can puncture a lung or other vital organs if left untreated, while a pneumothorax can lead to a tension pneumothorax, a life-threatening condition. If you suspect you have either condition, seek immediate medical care.

CHAPTER 24
OUR FALLS PREVENTION UK SURVEY

We contacted 100 local UK trainers, coaches and judges to ask for their feedback on how to prevent falls and to determine their best practices for training. All of them teach professional riders at high levels, and each has/or is currently training and competing themselves in British Dressage, British Eventing and British Showjumping.

We asked all participants to fill out this survey, and to sign consent and a data protection form. The results of the survey were illuminating and are illustrated below in some simple graphs.

Riders were asked ten questions:

Q1. How many falls have you had in your equestrian career?
Q2. How many falls have you witnessed as a professional trainer?
Q3. Do you always wear safety gear at home when practising (hat and back protection)?
Q4. If yes, what do you wear and why?
Q5. Have you had any major falls and describe why you fell?
Q6. Looking back at your falls history, could you have done anything differently?

Q7. Do you routinely include falls prevention exercises such as balance and strength work, Pilates/yoga in your weekly workout routines? If so, how often?

Q8. After a fall, who is involved in your recovery process? Medical team, family, coaches, other?

Q9. After a fall, how quickly would you normally see a medical professional and why? If not, why not? If yes, who?

Q10. In your opinion, what is the number one reason people tend to fall off horses?

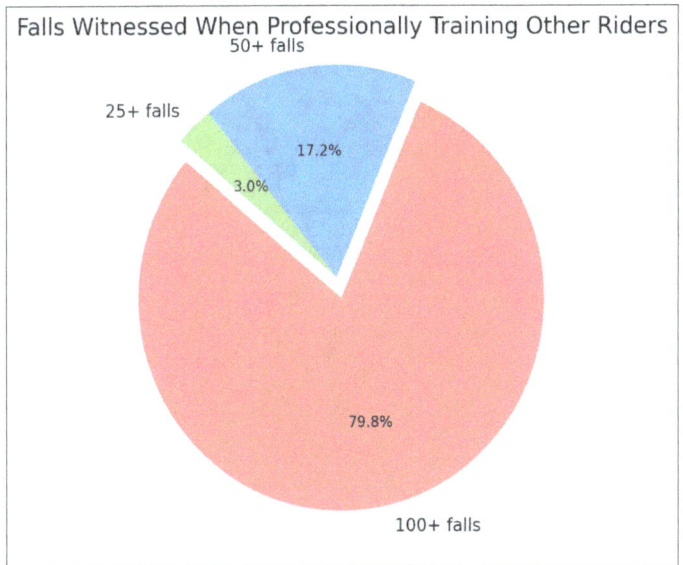

This pie chart illustrates the number of falls witnessed by professionals while training other riders. A significant majority, 79%, have observed more than 100 falls, highlighting the high risk of accidents in the sport, especially during professional training sessions.

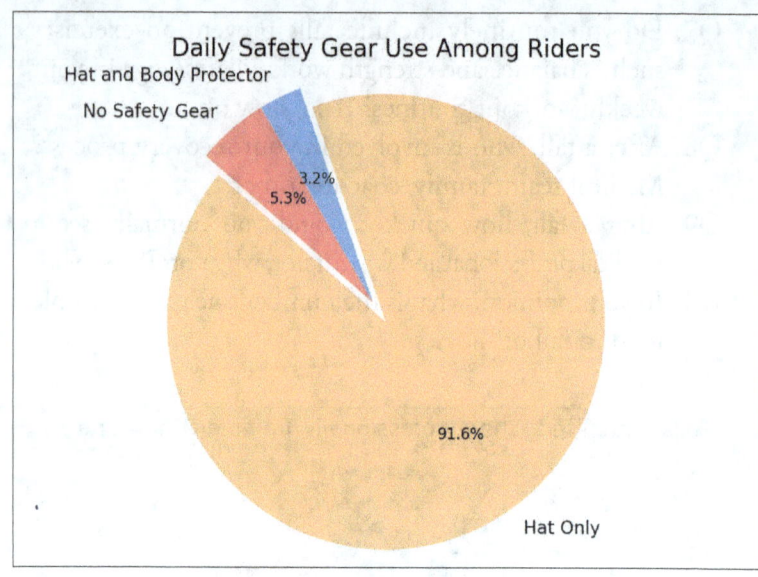

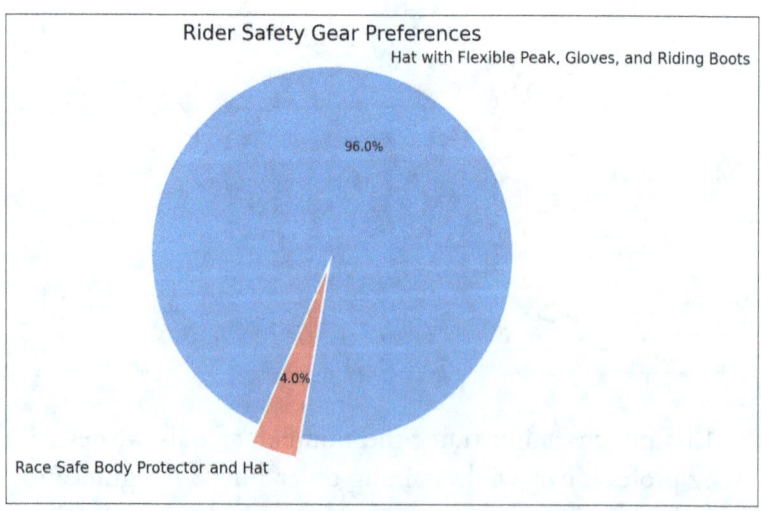

This pie chart depicts rider safety gear preferences. A vast majority, 96%, opt for a hat with a flexible peak along with gloves and riding boots, showcasing a preference for comprehensive yet specific types of protection. Only a small fraction, 4%, wear a race safe body protector in addition to a hat, highlighting varied priorities in safety gear choices among riders.

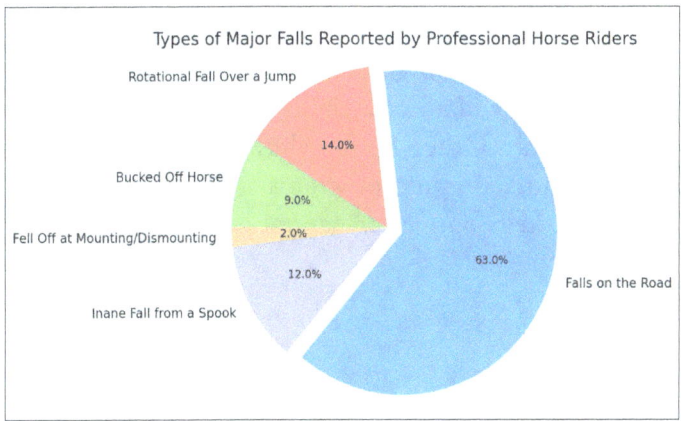

This pie chart displays the distribution of major fall types as reported by professional horse riders. It highlights that most falls occur on the road, making up 63% of the incidents. Other notable causes include rotational falls over jumps and being bucked off, alongside a smaller proportion of falls occurring during mounting/dismounting and due to being spooked.

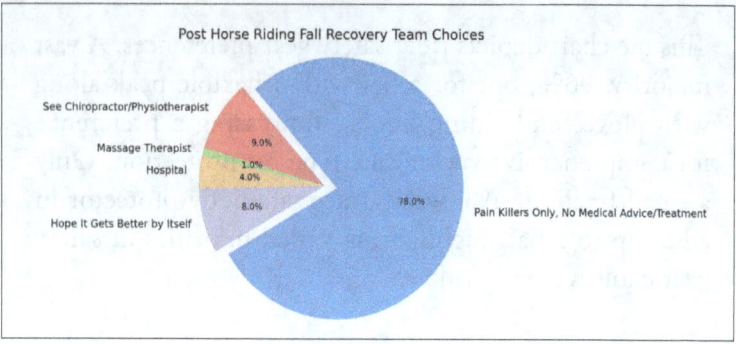

This pie chart highlights that a significant majority, 78%, opt for painkillers without seeking medical advice or treatment. Other approaches include consulting Chiropractors or physiotherapists, visiting hospitals, and some riders opting for natural recovery without any intervention.

CHAPTER 25

FEEDBACK AND ADVICE FROM THE PROFESSIONALS

We asked 100 UK professional trainers, judges, competitors and coaches, what advice they would give to equestrians to prevent falls.

"Be more relaxed: you can actually learn to fall using crash mats."

"Always roll away. Don't try to stop yourself falling by sticking your arms out!! Don't try to break your fall, I've seen many wrist fractures doing that. Keep your body tall, soft hands, look up. So many people rip forward or fold too early when jumping."

"Body tall at all times keeps you out of the danger zone." Caitlin Padfield, (Eventer & horse trainer).

"Ill prepared horses, especially young horses."

"Riders with unconscious incompetence, galloping down to a 4ft oxer."

"Being able to stay on a horse is about developing an independent seat, but the skill of not falling off is overall good horsemanship which encumbers above many things, good judgment. Strength can't hold you in the saddle, but a good core and symmetry in your weight in your seat, leg and hands will provide better balance." Fiona Mackinnon (Eventer, professional coach and judge).

"Road traffic safety and letting people know when you leave the yard." J Stephens (Judge and BD rider).

"Parents not seeking professional advice when buying new horses for their children. Over faced and under prepared for the job." D. Harland (BS and professional trainer and coach).

"Focus on the basics, develop symmetry in your body."

"Ride multiple horses if possible." D Harland (SJ and professional coach).

"Lack of commitment to a fence is a big reason for falls in my experience." Katie (BD, coach).

"Falls happen when there is a lack of fitness from horse/rider."
   "Stick to your limits." (Daniel, BD, Eventer).

"Never drop your hands before a fence. Horses can sense that you have dropped your contact and can then drop you instead." J Munro (Judge and professional coach).

"More knowledge and training." Caroline Rios (BS and professional coach).

"Experience and understanding." Blair-Wallace Stocks (BS and professional coach).

"Reflection: but decisions and actions are made in a split second." Jen Morris (Eventer and professional coach).

Thank you to everyone who took time out to help give feedback and advice.

CHAPTER 26
A FEW BIG THANK YOUS

It's day 14 now and I could walk without crutches after day 5, get dressed by myself and use the stairs without holding onto anything – result! I haven't needed any pain relief since day one, and I can sleep through the night without pain.

I would firstly like to thank my family for helping me out in the initial days of groans in agony, and for helping me function, like putting on my socks etc. It's a great way to feel like an old lady: when you are in a lot of pain.

A million thanks to our team of expert Chiropractors, sports massage therapists, acupuncturists, clinical psychologists, yoga and Pilates instructors and strength and conditioning coaches for healing me, at least 90% faster than I should have been. I wouldn't have been able to walk without you all!

Thank you to my team of instructors and mentors for their dedication and hours of coaching. Especially for refraining from rolling your eyes and laughing when I fall off.

Lastly, a big thank you to my horse, Blue, who despite many unintentional errors with his rider's performance, balance and seat, is still keen to do it all again. He is a one in a million partner and has taught me so much.

The kindness of others plays a crucial role in the healing process when we are in pain, both physically and emotionally. This compassion offers psychological comfort that can significantly reduce the perception of pain, fostering a positive and hopeful mindset essential for recovery. Such support not only alleviates feelings of isolation and despair, but also encourages adherence to treatment plans by instilling a sense of being cared for and understood. The emotional uplift that comes from kindness can trigger biological responses too, like the release of endorphins, which naturally dull pain and enhance well-being.

For medical professionals, especially Chiropractors, the motivation to help people achieve their wellness goals stems from a deep-seated desire to improve the quality of life for their patients. Witnessing the transformation in patients as they progress from pain and discomfort to mobility and wellness is profoundly rewarding.

Chiropractors are drawn to their field by the holistic approach to health it embodies—focusing not just on alleviating symptoms but on identifying and treating the root cause of discomfort. This process allows them to forge meaningful connections with patients, understanding their unique conditions and guiding them towards a healthier, more balanced lifestyle.

The joy and satisfaction derived from seeing patients reclaim their ability to enjoy life to the fullest, free from pain, are what fuel their passion and commitment to the field of chiropractic care.

I hope that this book has shown that Chiropractic, like physical therapy, is a profession and not a "technique". The benefits have been utilised by millions worldwide since 1895.

Choose a professional who works with you to achieve your goals. They will change your life!

CLOSING REMARKS

In conclusion, I hope this book can serve as a comprehensive guide for a horse rider or professional seeking to enhance safety, minimise the risk of falls and hopefully mitigate the potential for injury. By implementing the strategies outlined within these pages, you will not only gain a deeper understanding of the factors contributing to falls and tissue injury, but also acquire practical skills and knowledge to

navigate your equestrian pursuits with confidence and caution.

Remember, the journey towards safer riding begins with education, awareness and a commitment to continuous improvement. By learning from past mistakes, understanding the biomechanics of both horse and rider and adopting proactive safety measures, you can significantly reduce the likelihood of falls and safeguard your well-being in the saddle.

As you embark on your riding adventures, I encourage you to prioritise safety, listen to your instincts and never underestimate the importance of ongoing learning and growth. With dedication and diligence, you can enjoy the exhilaration of horse riding while minimising risks and ensuring a fulfilling and injury-free experience for both you and your equine partner.

> *Ride safe, ride smart, and may your equestrian journey be filled with joy, confidence, and endless possibilities.*

CHAPTER 27
REFERENCES FOR FURTHER READING

Ball, C. G., Ball, J. E., Kirkpatrick, A. W., & Mulloy, R. H. (2007). Equestrian injuries: Incidence, injury patterns, and risk factors for 10 years of major traumatic injuries. *The American Journal of Surgery, 193*(5), 636-640. doi.org/10.1016/j.amjsurg.2007.01.016

Bennet ED, Cameron-Whytock H, Parkin TDH. Fédération Equestre Internationale eventing: Risk factors for horse falls and unseated riders during the cross-country phase (2008-2018). Equine Vet J. 2022; 54: 885–894. https://doi.org/10.1111/evj.13522

Brachman, A., Kamieniarz, A., Michalska, J., Pawłowski, M., Słomka, K. J., & Juras, G. (2017). Balance Training Programs in Athletes – a Systematic Review. *Journal of Human Kinetics*, 58, 45–64. doi:10.1515/hukin-2017-0088.

Burke-Doe A, Hudson A, Werth H, Riordan DG. Knowledge of osteoporosis risk factors and prevalence of risk factors for osteoporosis, falls, and fracture in functionally independent older adults. J Geriatr Phys Ther. 2008;31(1):11–17

Butterwick, D. J., Hagel, B., Nelson, D. S., LeFave, M. R., & Meeuwisse, W. H. (2002). Epidemiologic analysis of injury in five years of Canadian professional rodeo. *American Journal of Sports Medicine, 30*(2), 193-198. doi.org/10.1177/03635465020300020801

Delzo, J. (2016). The oldest and youngest Olympic athletes. *Olympic Games 2016*. Retrieved from cnn.com/2016/08/11/health/youngest-and-oldest-olympic-athletes/

Edmonds, C., & Next Avenue. (2015). The Steep Cost of Brain Injury Recovery.

Fernanda Camargo, William R. Gombeski Jr, Polly Barger, Connie Jehlik, Holly Wiemers, James Mead & Amy Lawyer | Pedro González-Redondo (Reviewing Editor) (2018). Horse-related injuries: Causes, preventability, and where educational efforts should be focused, *Cogent Food & Agriculture, 4*(1), DOI: 10.1080/23311932.2018.1432168.

Gizzi, M., Christie, L., Croker, W., & Crowe, P. (2003). Pattern of equestrian injuries presenting to a Sydney teaching hospital. *ANZ Journal of Surgery, 73*(8), 567-571.

Guyton, K., Houchen-Wise, E., Peck, E., & Mayberry, J. (2013). Equestrian Injury is Costly, Disabling, and Frequently Preventable: The Imperative for Improved Safety Awareness.

Hughes, K. M., Falcone, R. E., Price, J., & Witkoff, M. (1995). Equestrian-related trauma. *The American Journal of Emergency Medicine, 13*(4), 485-487. doi.org/10.1016/0735-6757(95)90148-5

Ikinger, C. M., Baldamus, J., & Spiller, A. (2016). Factors influencing the safety behaviour of German equestrians: Attitudes towards protective equipment and peer behaviours. *Animals, 6*(2), 14. doi.org/10.3390/ani6020014

Leandro dos Santos et al (2016) Sarcopenia and physical independence in older adults: the independent and synergic role of muscle mass and muscle function

Leslie J Roberts, Michael McVeigh, +4 authors D. Szmulewicz (2002), Overview of the Clinical Approach to Individuals With Cerebellar Ataxia and Neuropathy, Neurology: Genetics 28.

Mastellar, S. L. (2020). Equestrian Injury Statistics.

Mutore, K., Lim, J., Fofana, D., et al (2021). Hearing hoofbeats? Think head and neck trauma: a 10-year NTDB analysis of equestrian-related trauma in the USA. *Trauma Surgery & Acute Care Open, 6*(1), e000728. doi: 10.1136/tsaco-2021-000728. CC BY-NC 4.0

NICE Guidelines for low back pain and sciatica NG59, 2016

Silver, J. Spinal injuries resulting from horse riding accidents. Spinal Cord 40, 264–271 (2002). https://doi.org/10.1038/sj.sc.3101280

Sorli, J. M. (2000). Equestrian injuries: a five-year review of hospital admissions in British Columbia, Canada. *Injury Prevention, 6*, 59-61.

Stanfill, A. G., Wynja, K., Cao, X., Prescott, D., Shore, S., Baughman, B., Oddo, A., & Tsao, J. W. (2020). Helmet use in equestrian athletes: opportunities for intervention.

Stephens, J.M., Sharpe, K., Gore, C., Miller, J., Slater, G.J., Versey, N., Peiffer, J., Duffield, R., Minett, G.M., Crampton, D., Dunne, A., Askew, C.D., & Halson, S.L. (2018). Core temperature responses to cold-water immersion recovery: a pooled-data analysis. International Journal of Sports Physiology and Performance, 13, 917-925.

Thomas, K. E., Annest, J. L., Gilchrist, J., & Bixby-Hammett, D. M. (2006). Non-fatal horse related injuries treated in emergency departments in the United States, 2001-2003. *Br J Sports Med, 40*(7), 619-26. doi: 10.1136/bjsm.2006.025858. PMID: 16611723; PMCID: PMC2564310.

Walsh J, Hoffstad O, Sullivan M, Margolis D. 2016 Association of diabetic foot ulcer and death in a population-based cohort from the United Kingdom. Diabet. Med. 33, 1493-1498. (doi:10.1111/dme.13054)

Winkler, E. A., Yue, J. K., Burke, J. F., Chan, A. K., Dhall, S. S., Berger, M. S., Manley, G. T., & Tarapore, P. E. (2016). Adult sports-related traumatic brain injury in United States trauma centers.

Wong SL, Demers M, Martinod K, Gallant M, Wang Y, Goldfine AB, Kahn CR, Wagner DD. 2015 Diabetes primes neutrophils to undergo NETosis, which impairs wound healing. Nat. Med. 21, 815-819.

CHAPTER 28
HOW TO GET IN TOUCH FOR A CONSULTATION

Scan the QR Code when you want to visit us in person or book a virtual consultation from the comfort of your home.

Our Clinical Locations:
- Riverside Chiropractic Clinic, 581-585 Holburn Street, Aberdeen, Scotland, UK
- Westhill Business Centre, Aberdeenshire
- Aberdeenshire Chiropractic Clinic, Oldmeldrum

Book now

Call 📞 01224 211517